KOVELS' BID, BUY, AND SELL ONLINE

Kovels'
Bid, Buy, and Sell Online

BASIC AUCTION INFORMATION

and TRICKS of the TRADE

Ralph and Terry Kovel

THREE RIVERS PRESS
NEW YORK

Copyright © 2001 by Ralph and Terry Kovel

Published by Three Rivers Press, New York, New York.
Member of the Crown Publishing Group.

Random House, Inc. New York, Toronto, London, Sydney, Auckland
www.randomhouse.com

THREE RIVERS PRESS is a registered trademark and the
Three Rivers Press colophon is a trademark of Random House, Inc.

Printed in the United States of America

Design by Karen Minster

Library of Congress Cataloging-in-Publication Data
Kovel, Ralph M.
    Kovel's bid, buy, and sell online: basic auction information and tricks of the trade / by Ralph and Terry Kovel—1st ed.
    1. Internet auctions.   I. Title: Bid, buy, and sell online.
    II. Kovel, Terry H.   III. Title.
HF5478.K68   2001
381'.17'02854678—dc21   00-046589

ISBN 0-609-80757-9

10 9 8 7 6 5 4 3 2 1

First Edition

To all the collectors
who chase their dreams in the
Internet auctions and malls.

And to whoever it was
who actually invented
the Internet.

Contents

Acknowledgments

COMPUTER PEOPLE SPEAK A SPECIAL LANGUAGE that must be translated for those just learning the world of PCs. This book needed both the experts and the beginners. Our thanks go to Marcia Goldberg and Karen Kneisley, who visited Web sites, interviewed dealers and collectors who were buying and selling online, and reviewed and revised many sections of the book. Thanks also to Amy Garvey, who added her light-hearted charm to some of our explanations. And heartfelt thanks to Kim Kovel, our online expert. She transformed "mystery" into "understandable," so that our readers can feel comfortable chasing collectibles online.

After the first draft of the book, we asked some neophytes to follow the directions and learned that it was confusing to call a rectangle a "button" and even that a true beginner didn't know what we meant by "click." We thank them for their questions and suggestions and for their bravery in trying the Internet for the first time. And a special thank-you to our editor, Dottie Harris, who masterminded the design, the cover, and all the other details that made this book what it is.

We also wish to thank the dealer mall and online auctions that gave us permission to include screen shots from their Web sites in this book. The following list includes the people who helped us at each company, along with the screen-shot permission notice each requested: Heather Peterson at Amazon.com (Copyright © Amazon.com Inc., All Rights Reserved); Elizabeth Compton at America Online (Netscape software toolbar icons © 2000 Netscape Communications Corp. Used with permission); Staci L. Kay at eBay (These materials have been reproduced with the permission of eBay Inc. Copyright © eBay Inc. All Rights Reserved); Philip Davies at The Internet Antique Shop (Copyright © TIAS Inc., All Rights Reserved); and Jami Heldt at Yahoo (Reproduced with permission of Yahoo! Inc. © 2000 by Yahoo! Inc. YAHOO! and the YAHOO! logo are trademarks of Yahoo! Inc.).

Introduction

AT EVERY AUCTION GALLERY, show, shop, or mall we walk into, we hear about Internet auctions. It started with eBay, but now there are many more, including Amazon, Yahoo, and eHammer. Here we give you the basic information you'll need to make online buys at good prices and to put your items into an online auction. You'll learn successful bidding strategies and auction tips we've used ourselves.

In addition, you'll find a list of Web sites for online auctions, antiques malls, price lists including—of course—*Kovels' Online Price Guide* (www.kovels.com), research information, image (photo) hosts, online appraisers, auction-search services, and other related sites. Auction-search services "spider" (automatically search) several ongoing online auctions to locate the specific collectible you want to buy. Some auction sites bar spidering, but you may still find the search services helpful. Although our lengthy list of Web sites is accurate today, new sites are appearing all the time and some sites may have disappeared. Check the up-to-the-minute list on our own Web site (www.kovels.com).

This book is arranged into three major parts. Part One is written for collectors who have just gotten their first computer and need a friend to help them turn it on.

In Part Two, you'll learn how to register at an online auction site, how to find what you want to buy, bidding rules, the pitfalls of some payment methods, and warnings about fakes and fraud.

If you want to sell online, jump to Part Three. There we tell you where you can sell your item, how to word your ad so you can find the most buyers and get the best prices, how to use photos online, the various shipping methods you can use, and how to avoid problems, including fraud.

Near the beginning of the book is a list of the general rules of Internet etiquette (called "Netiquette"), and near the end is a glossary of cyberspace terms and a review of various antiques and collectibles that have sold through online auctions. Also included in the book are two auction diaries kept by a buyer and seller during a real online auction. Finally, we include a chart comparing the fees, rules, and practices of the three largest Internet auctions: eBay, Amazon, and Yahoo.

NOTE: The information included in this book
was accurate at the time of publication.
Readers should be aware that computer technology
and Web site designs are constantly changing.

PART ONE

Guide for Computer Neophytes

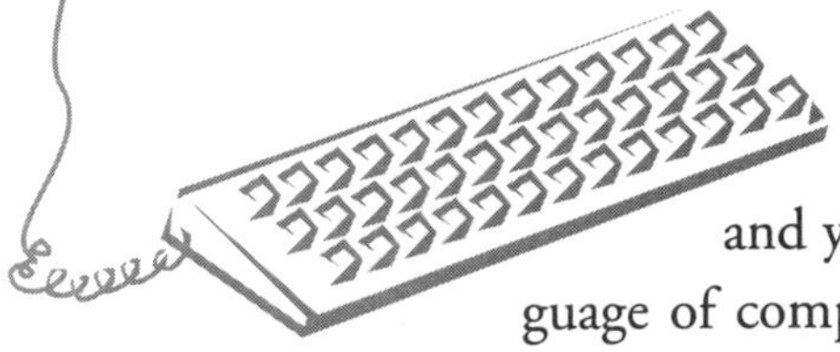

IF YOU JUST BOUGHT YOUR first computer and modem and you're not familiar with the language of computers, relax. Your computer is the machine that starts your journey to an online auction. The modem (or network card, if you have access to a network or broadband service) is the "car" that takes you over the "road" of your phone line or cable connection. To access the Internet's online auctions, your computer must be hooked up to a phone line, cable connection, or network, and you must subscribe to an Internet Service Provider (ISP). The ISP will probably charge a monthly fee. Once you are online, there are other terms you'll need to know:

Screens & Pages

The *screen* is everything you see on your computer's monitor. The *page,* when you are on the Internet, is displayed in the central boxed part of the screen. You may need to *scroll* down (use your mouse to pull the sliding rectangle on the scroll bar on the right side of the screen) to see the rest of the page.

Buttons & Underlined Words on Your Internet Browser

To move around on the Internet, you have to tell your computer what to do. Sometimes the words on a page will ask you to enter information in a box. Next to the box is a *button* that may be a colored circle, rectangle, or odd shape. To make the computer use the information you typed in the box, you need to click on the button. Sometimes the page gives you colored, bold, or underlined words to choose from. The words link you to another page on that site or to another site. To get to one of those pages, click on the highlighted words, called *links*. If an hourglass appears, just wait. It is telling you your computer is working but has not yet finished its task.

What's at the Top of the Screen?

Across the top of the screen is a toolbar with symbols that also act as *buttons*. By clicking on either the symbols or words, you can print, go to your home page, send e-mail, and much more. Beware—the buttons on the top of the screen take you to differ-

GENERAL RULES OF "NETIQUETTE"

↗ Do not type words in all capital letters.
   It's considered yelling.

↗ Keep your messages and e-mails brief. Time is too important to waste reading messages that don't get to the point.

↗ If you are replying to someone's e-mail, click the "Reply" button or copy that person's e-mail into your own e-mail message. It's an easy way to keep track of questions and answers. If you are replying to a very long e-mail, copy just the section you're answering or retype the question in your answer.

↗ Be courteous. You don't want to be accused of "flaming"—being abusive with words. Some people who are rarely rude in person find it easy to slip into unacceptable language when they're sitting in front of a computer screen. Don't let your supposed anonymity lead you to behave badly. You can guard against this by reading over your e-mail, chat room, or bulletin board message before sending it. If you do regret sending a particular message, apologize immediately.

ent places than the buttons on a Web page. Those buttons take you backward or forward on the site's pages, or stop the *loading* of a page.

Where Am I?

You've clicked so many things, you don't recognize the pages anymore. Just click on the back arrow (usually at the top left corner of the screen) until you get back to a familiar page.

Internet Browser Terms

©2000 Netscape Communications Corp.

MENU BAR: The row of words under the browser title at the top of your computer screen, whether you're using Netscape, Microsoft Internet Explorer, or America Online's browser. The words usually include: File, Edit, View, Go, Options, Favorites (or Bookmarks), and Help. Each of these buttons allows you to work with your browser in various ways—you can open, close, cut, copy, paste, move from page to page, and get help by clicking on these words.

©2000 Netscape Communications Corp.

TOOLBAR: The row of picture buttons under the menu bar. It varies from browser to browser, but usually includes the following:

BACK: Takes you to the page you had open before the one you're now on.

FORWARD: Returns you to the page you were on before you hit the "Back" button.

STOP: Stops the loading of the current page. Most people use this if the page is not the one they meant to load or if the information wanted comes up on the page before the page has completely loaded. Hitting the "Stop" button can save you time.

REFRESH OR RELOAD: Click on this button (sometimes a circular arrow), and you reload the current page. This is helpful if you are following an ongoing auction or want to see the latest postings on a bulletin board.

HOME: This button takes you back to the page that comes up when you open your browser. You can set your home page to whatever URL (Uniform Resource Locator, or a Web site address) you like.

SEARCH OR FIND: This button is either on your toolbar or is an option you can place there. Click on it and you can search the Internet for information on whatever subject interests you. What you're actually doing is accessing several popular search engines, such as Google, Lycos, or Yahoo.

PRINT: Click on the little printer icon and the page on your screen prints out on your printer.

©2000 Netscape
Communications Corp.

There are other computer, Internet, and browser terms you should become familiar with. Learn how to clean out your cache, how to read a Web site address, and how to understand error messages.

Regularly cleaning your ISP's cache will keep your computer running at its optimal speed when you're online. Just click on your ISP's Help screen and look for "cache" to learn how to do it. If you use AOL, for example, you clean the cache by following these steps: click "My AOL" at the top of the screen, select "Preferences," and click "WWW." Under the "General" tab, click

"Delete Files" under "Temporary Internet Files"; under "History," click "Clear History." Also click the "Settings" button under "Temporary Internet Files" and reduce the "amount of disk space to use" to store Web graphics to about 50MB. A large cache file can slow you down.

If you type a URL in your browser's location bar and hit your enter key, but the site does not come up, you may see one of the following error messages:

1. **404 Not Found: The requested URL was not found on this server.** This means that your browser found the Internet service or computer hosting the Web site you're looking for, but not the page whose address you typed. The very last "word" (often htm or html) at the end of a URL is the page's address. If the last word is htm, try html, and vice versa. If that doesn't work, delete the portion of the address beyond the home page, so the site you're looking for ends, simply, in .com, .org, .gov, or .edu.

2. **DNS Lookup Failure.** DNS is an acronym for Domain Name Server. A domain name is the part of the URL that follows the www. and ends with .com (or .org, etc.). The domain name may no longer exist, or maybe it is too new to be found on any database your server accesses. This message can also come up if there is heavy traffic on the Internet. Try again later in the day or week. If you still can't bring up the domain name, it probably doesn't exist.

3. **No response from server.** Your Internet browser was unable to get a timely response from the Web site's host computer. This can be caused by heavy

traffic on the Internet, on your ISP, or on the host. Try again later.

4 **Server is busy.** This message is posted by heavily trafficked sites. Try again later.

PART TWO

Buying on the Internet

INTERNET AUCTIONS GET the most publicity, but you don't have to use an auction to buy online. Many "brick-and-mortar" antiques malls and shops are now selling online, too. Or you could find what you're looking for at a "virtual" mall or shop that sells only over the Internet. The Internet Antique Shop (www.tias.com), for example, is an online mall of dealers (some of whom also have real shops) who sell their products to Internet shoppers.

TIAS home page.

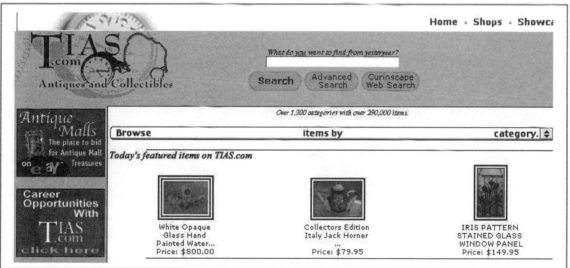

Buying from a dealer's shop online is much like buying by mail through a catalog or advertisement. In both cases, the price is set by the dealer, you pay the price plus shipping, and the dealer ships you your purchase. In both cases, don't be afraid to call or e-mail the dealer to bargain for a lower price. Perhaps you want to order two pieces of Depression glass rather than one; the dealer might give you a bargain price if you order both at once. The dealer must follow federal laws relating to mail orders, and you, the buyer, must be sure that the shipment is insured.

Let's Tour an Internet Auction Site

There are many Internet auction sites. The best known is eBay (www.ebay.com), but other online auctions, such as Amazon and Yahoo, work much the same way. Most online auctions operate a lot like live antiques auctions. If you're familiar with the way live auctions work—raising paddles or waving hands at an auctioneer, absentee bidding, and bidding strategies—you'll quickly become comfortable with online auctions. If bidding at any kind of an auction is new to you, get ready to have some fun.

Getting to an Internet Auction

To visit an online auction, you must have a computer with a modem or network card that is hooked to a communications system (like a phone line, cable connection, or network), plus an Internet service provider (ISP). America Online, Prodigy, AT&T WorldNet, Mindspring, Earthlink, and Microsoft Network are well-known ISPs, but there are many more. New computers usually come loaded with at least one ISP's software. If your computer has no ISP software, you'll have to order a disk or CD-ROM from a provider. In some parts of the country, phone and cable television companies offer special high-speed connections to the Internet; some even offer browser software.

Most ISPs provide easy access to an Internet browser. If you are not happy using that browser, however, you can download the one you prefer. AOL users, for example, can go to Netscape's Web site and download the Netscape browser.

Once you have an ISP, take this book over to your computer and follow along with us. Double-click on the icon for your ISP, then sign on. When you get online, you can click on the Internet icon if your ISP has one, or you can skip that step and go right to the next one: type in a Web site's address (URL) in the long, narrow, white box (the locator bar) on the screen, then hit your keyboard's "Enter" key or click the "Go" button next to the locator bar.

Web sites have addresses just as houses do. That's because a Web site is a "place" out in cyberspace. For example, you can get to eBay's Web site address by typing in: www.ebay.com.

Locator bar

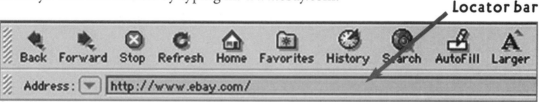

© 2000 Netscape Communications Corp.

Be sure you type every letter and punctuation mark correctly. One error and you will be at another "house," or your computer will display a screen that tells you the site you typed does not exist or cannot be reached.

When you reach a Web site, the screen that appears first is called a "home page." On eBay's home page, you might want to click "New to eBay?" at the top right and read the introductory lessons listed on the page. They're listed like a table of contents, which you read by scrolling down with the help of the arrows or the button on the scroll bar at the right side of your screen. You go to each lesson by clicking your mouse on the highlighted words (links) on the screen. The links are usually highlighted by color and underlining, but if you aren't sure which words are links, look at your mouse's arrow as you move around the screen. The arrow turns into a hand with a pointing finger when it touches a link. Any time you want to get back to the home page, you can click the back arrow at the top left of the page or the link on the screen that says "Home Page" or "Home." Keep in mind, by the way, that Web sites frequently change their graphics or links, so get used to finding new colors, words, and information on all your favorite sites, including eBay. And don't be surprised if a new banner ad suddenly appears on your screen. It's all part of Internet marketing.

You don't have to *register* (fill out an on-screen form with your name, address, and other information) to look at eBay's instructions or auction listings. You do have to register to buy and sell things, and sellers must include a credit card number in their registration forms. (Some auction sites, such as Amazon, require both buyers and sellers to submit a credit card number.)

If you want to look around (browse) the auction site without buying or selling, choose a category from the alphabetical list on

EBay home page.

Search bar   **Search button**

the left side of the home page—try "Collectibles"—and click on it. The page you go to next lists subcategories. After you click on a subcategory, a longer page comes up that lists current auction items. Scroll down using your mouse either to click the down arrow or drag the sliding rectangle on the scroll bar on right side of the screen. To view details about the item you like, click on the underlined words.

Search bar

Amazon.com Auctions home page.

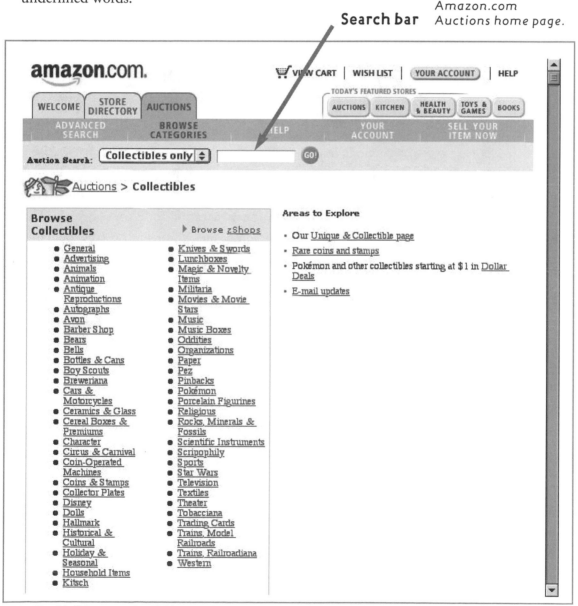

Another way to find things is to *search*. Type a word (such as "Bakelite") into the box next to the search button. There's a search button on the home page and on other pages, too. Click the button and a page will come up with auction descriptions that contain the word you typed. Search methods vary from site to site, so for more detailed instructions on search methods, click on the word "Help" or "Tips" next to the search button on the auction site.

Registration to Buy or Sell

If you're going to buy or sell collectibles online, you need to go to the auction's "registration" page and follow the instructions. On the auction's home page, click on the word "Register." A warning about sending information over the Internet will appear. Read it and click on the answer you prefer (whether to hide the box in the future or not). Fill in the registration form on the page. (This is a time-consuming and sometimes annoying process, but once you have registered at an auction site, you don't have to register again no matter how many times you buy or sell.)

When you register, you are asked for your full name, complete street address, daytime and evening phone numbers, fax number if you have one, e-mail address, and your company name (if you are buying or selling as a business). You also have to choose a "user name" for yourself (also called a "user ID") and a password. (Some auctions e-mail you a confirmation number, then ask you to choose a password when you confirm your registration. At the same time, you should read the auction's user agreement so you understand the rules of the auction site.)

Registration is free. Be sure you write down your user name and password—you will use them every time you want to buy or sell on the auction Web site. Bidders usually choose user names unrelated to their real names so they can bid anonymously; many simply use their e-mail address. Your user name is the name others will see when you bid and when you sell. Your password should be something you can remember easily but that can't be easily guessed by others. It is the "lock" that prevents someone else from going to the auction site and acting for you.

---

ebaY™

| Browse | Sell | Services | Search | Help | Community |

eBay Registration

Welcome! Let's begin.

- Please enter your required contact information below

Note: You must be at least 18 years old to register on eBay.

Enter your contact Information	
Email address	required Note: Enter your valid email address - including your "@serviceprovider.com" domain. For example, if your AOL screen name is joe cool, your email address is joecool@aol.com
Full name e.g., John H. Doe	required First M. Last
Company	optional
Address	required
City	required
State	Select State ▼ required
Zip	required
Primary phone # e.g., (408) 555 - 1234	( ) - Extension: required
Secondary phone #	( ) - Extension: optional

When you click "Register" on the eBay home page, you reach a screen that says you must be 18 years old to register and asks you what country you live in. Once you highlight your country, click the bar that says "Continue." It brings up the eBay registration page above. You must complete the form on this page to be a registered eBay user. Once you have registered, every time you go to eBay's site to buy or sell, you can click the "Sign in" link at the top of eBay's home page and enter your user ID and password. If you don't sign in but try to buy or sell, you will be asked for your user ID and password.

You must register at EACH auction site you use. The user name and password you used to register on eBay will not allow you to use Amazon's Web site, for example. You can, however, choose to use the same user name and password at each site.

BASIC TYPES OF INTERNET AUCTIONS

There are hundreds of Internet auctions of antiques and collectibles, but there are only a few basic auction types:

Person-to-person: Amazon, eBay, and Yahoo are called "person-to-person" auctions because they link one person selling something to another person who buys it. The buyer pays the seller, not the auction. The seller pays the auction a fee.

Consignment: People with items to sell consign them to an auction, and buyers go online to bid on the items. This is the way many traditional live auctions as well as longtime mail and phone auctions are using the Internet to reach buyers. The auctions put their catalogs online, and some allow you to e-mail your bids. In this sort of auction, your e-mail bid is treated as though it were a phone bid. Sotheby's, the famous auction house, uses its Web site, www.sothebys.com, to offer a wide range of consigned items to online bidders. You can also use the Web site to view Sotheby's live-auction catalogs. But you cannot bid online for items in the live auctions. There are also online specialty auctions that sell everything from postcards (www.ilovepostcards.com) to marbles (www.blocksite.com/chip).

Live auctions and Web bids: Some Internet auctions and some traditional auctions are using "Web-cast" technology to accept live-auction bids online. You stay online, follow the auction, and use a bidding form on the auction's Web site to submit your bids in real time. It can be compared to bidding by phone during a live auction or acting as your own "absentee" bidder.

ATTENDING A LIVE AUCTION ONLINE

Several Web sites exist that allow bidders to hear the auctioneer and be part of the action. If you have an itch to try this out, do some prep work:

Preview the items. To avoid getting swept up in auction fever, preview the items well before the auction and decide what you want to bid on and how much you will pay. Write down auction item numbers and details. If you have any questions, contact the auction house.

Practice bidding. Some auction sites offer a simulator for you to practice your bidding technique. Do it so you don't flub it during the real thing.

Remember, it's not perfect. The auctioneer's voice may sound garbled, the pictures may not match up with the auction action, and the bids listed may not be up-to-the-minute. It's simply the nature of the beast. Technology will progress, though.

Be patient. If you're not sure at the close that you won an item, you'll have to wait for the auction house to post the winning bids or contact you. This may take up to a week.

Buyer's premium. Internet person-to-person auctions like eBay and eHammer do not normally charge a buyer's premium. A buyer's premium is a fee (usually 10–15 percent of the buyer's winning bid) charged to the buyer by the auction itself, not by the seller. Most traditional live and mail-phone auctions do charge a buyer's premium, even if you bid online.

Each item listed on an online auction site is offered in an individual auction that lasts a few days. The ending time of each auction is listed for each item. The methods of payment the seller will accept (check, money order, credit card) and the shipping costs the seller will charge should also be listed.

Eyes in the Back of Your Head

Hopping from site to site to find items you want to bid on can be time-consuming. Auction search services, nicknamed "spiders," exist that will do the shopping for you. The downside: The search mechanisms can be confusing to use, and some auction sites are trying through legal action to bar them. Sites that spider include: AuctionRover (www.auctionrover.com), E-compare (www.ecompare.com/index-auction.html), Bidder's Edge (www.biddersedge.com), Auction Watch (www.auctionwatch.com), and TelliTrack (www.itrack.com).

EBay search screen.

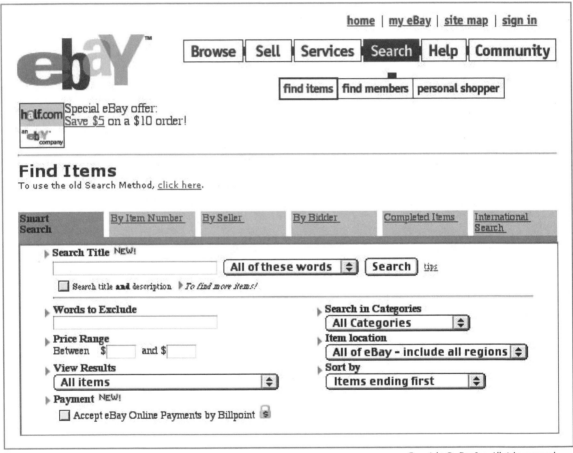

Searching an Online Auction for the Thing You Want to Buy

Nearly all online auctions include a search feature that allows you to type in the name of an item you're looking for. Be sure you read the rules for using each site's search option. Consider how a seller might list what you're looking for. For example, if you're at eBay's site and you're looking for a pink creamer in the Adam pattern of Depression glass, you can assume that any seller would include at least the words "Adam creamer" in the auction title. So those are the words you enter in the search box. You can try other combinations, too, such as: "Adam Depression pink creamer." Some online auctions allow you to search item descriptions as well as titles; eBay, for example, allows you to click on a box that says, "Search title and description." You can do more sophisticated and narrow searches by following the search tips available on the auction site.

SEARCH TECHNIQUES

There are several other ways you can search for items at online auction sites. Most auctions allow you to:

1. Browse categories and subcategories, which is much like leafing through an auction catalog.

2. Search by seller's user name. (Why would you want to do this? Perhaps because you bought from this seller before and know he or she is trustworthy, or perhaps because you know this seller is auctioning a lot of your favorite kind of collectible.)

3. Search by bidder's user name. (Perhaps you discovered that another bidder is always shopping for the same things you want to buy. You can follow that bidder's trail with this search method. Or perhaps you are bidding on so many things at the same time that you have lost track of your own bids.)

4. Search by auction number. (Every auction offered on the site has its own number, which is listed alongside the auction title. If you are interested in that item, jot down the number and search using it to check on how the auction is going.)

5. Search only ongoing auctions, auctions ending today, or completed auctions. (Searching completed auctions shows you the realized prices of items similar to those you want to buy. It can also help sellers figure out the price they should set as an opening bid.)

SPELL CHEK

If you can't seem to find what you're looking for, check your spelling. Check it again. "Limoge" is not going to take you to "Limoges"—though it will take you to the seller who can't spell well, and may get you a deal! For example, if you wanted the 1991 Stadium Club rookie card for Green Bay Packer quarterback Brett Favre, you might go with the most common misspelling of his name, "Farve." That's the spelling Stadium Club used.

Always consider other possible misspellings when you're searching. Watch for the incorrect Wedgewood (it should be Wedgwood), Sheridan (Sheraton), Severs (Sevres), Hisey (Heisey), Britain (Britains), dalmation (dalmatian), transister (transistor), Cambell (Campbell), nickle (nickel), millenium (millennium), M.J. Hummel (M.I. Hummel), Mickey Mantel (Mickey Mantle), Royal Dalton (Royal Doulton), majelica (majolica), Lennox (Lenox), Russell Right (Russel Wright), and even Chip n Dale (Chippendale). Then there are words like Jade-ite (Jadeite, Jadite) that were spelled different ways by different factories, words like *collectable* and *collectible* that are both right, and words like millefiori and chinoiserie that are just plain hard to spell.

Most search engines, including eBay's and Amazon's, accept capital or small (upper or lower case) letters interchangeably. So whether you search for "Depression glass" or "depression glass," you call up the same entries.

Use the singular rather than plural form of the item you're looking for. Type "creamer" instead of "creamers." Most sellers list items that way. You could search first using the word "creamer," then try again with "creamers" to find anything you might have missed.

Don't overlook alternative names or nicknames in your search. You'll find Mark Twain items listed under Samuel Clemens and Boston Red Sox memorabilia under Bosox. Even cities have nicknames. San Francisco becomes Frisco or San Fran; Philadelphia is called Philly.

Search Results

After you ask an auction search engine to search for a specific item, a list of results shows up on your computer screen. At the top is a message telling you how many listings were found. If there are a large number, you may be given tips on how to narrow your search.

Yahoo results for "doll auction" search.

YAHOO! Auctions

Yahoo! Auctions

Search Results for **doll**

| $30.00 | $45.00 | $15.00 | $15.75 | $18.00 |

Category Listing   Title Only   Description Only

Category Search Results (3 items)

Auctions > Antiques, Art, & Collectibles > Cultures & Groups > Religion & Spirituality > Voodoo > Dolls

Auctions > Toys, Games, & Hobbies > Dolls

Auctions > Toys, Games, & Hobbies > Dolls > Barbies > Dolls

Title Search Results (17182 items)

[Show only photos] [Show closed auctions]   Sort by: Photo | Title | Price | Bids | Time Left
Showing 1 of 344 pages(17182 items total)   Previous 50 | Next 50

Photo	Title	Price	Bids	Time Left
	Featured Auctions (more info)			
	HERITAGE SIGNATURE COLLECTION PORCELAIN DOLL	$9.99	-	7 days
	-=Sailor Moon Stars Dream Pocket Doll of SAILOR PLUTO Mint in Box=- *RARE* NEW!	$30.00	-	4 days
	Brand New Classic Traditional China Doll Chinese Woman 1st Bid Wins! ~ DUTCH	$19.95	1	3 days
	ALEXA INTERACTIVE DIVA STARZ DOLL BUY PRICE NO WAITING NO RESERVE	$45.00	-	5 days
	DUCK HOUSE HEIRLOOM 16" PORCELAIN DOLL	$15.00	-	23 hrs
	Indian Doll Long Black Hair NEW!	$15.75	-	1 day
	25" Beautiful Blonde Wedding Doll. MINT!!!!	$50.00	3	2 days
	Native American Porcelain Doll - Brand New	$25.95	-	8 days

The results usually include the auction number, title, whether or not the description includes a photo, the current high bid, the starting and ending dates for the auction, and the time left to place a bid.

Is It What You Want to Buy?

Once you've found your collectible, read the seller's description carefully to learn size, condition, color, etc. You can print the listing and study it. Watch for words like "refurbished" and "repaired." If the description is vague, if it doesn't say how old the item is, how big it is, or what condition it's in, e-mail the seller and ask. (A link to the seller's e-mail address is listed with the item. Click on the words: "Ask seller a question.") "Excellent condition" may mean one thing to the seller and another to you. Ask if the item is chipped, cracked, damaged, in working order, if it has all its parts, and if it has been repaired or repainted. Ask if the seller knows who owned it before. The history of an antique's ownership—its *provenance*—can add value.

Some descriptions are ambiguous. If a diamond ring is listed as "two-carat" and there is no photo or the photo is unclear, be sure you know how many diamonds are in the ring. One two-carat stone is much more valuable than ten stones that add up to two carats. If a Roseville vase is pictured with a mark that says, "same mark as this one from Kovels' book," don't assume that the Kovels have authenticated the piece or even that the piece is real. Last year we were told about some online auctions of Roseville pottery vases in which each vase was pictured, described, and its mark shown. Another picture showed a photocopy of the Roseville mark on a page in *Kovels' New Dictionary of Marks*. The caption said the mark was used "circa 1930." The mark caption was true, but the vase was a reproduction marked with a *copy* of the old mark. We could not stop the seller from using this devious format. Beware. Read descriptions carefully. If something is too good to be true, it usually is.

If you e-mail your questions to the seller, most sellers will e-mail back immediately, perhaps hoping that if you know more, you will pay more. Some sellers are unsophisticated, or at least uninitiated in the world of antiques and collectibles. They may call an item made in the 1970s an "antique." You must depend on your own knowledge when you buy. And you must ask the right questions. *If you e-mail the seller and get no response, or don't get the response you want, DO NOT BID.*

Once your questions are answered, but before you bid, consider the minimum bid requested by the seller. Is it well below current market value? Of course, if you own a copy of this year's edition of our book *Kovels' Antiques & Collectibles Price List,* you can look up current retail market prices quickly. Most sellers list a minimum bid well below market value (traditional auctions usually set minimum bids at one-third of market value). That's because a minimum bid set too close to market value scares bidders away.

WARNING SIGNS

Stay away from items or sales you learn about through bulk e-mail. Statistics show your chance of receiving the item is a measly 45 percent, and the chance of your being happy with what you do get (if you get it) is less than 5 percent.

Be wary of sellers who use free e-mail services such as Hotmail, Bigfoot, Excite, or Yahoo. It's easier for sellers to hide their real identities with a free service. And if the seller doesn't tell you his real name when you ask via e-mail, don't bid. A reputable seller will reveal his or her identity. (EBay and other auction sites now allow you to request another user's real identity and city—though not the user's street address—through a link on the site rather than by a personal e-mail.)

On big-ticket items, avoid sellers who refuse to use an escrow service.

Photographs

Most sellers provide a photograph of the item along with the description. If the collectible is a piece of pottery, glass, furniture, or anything else that has a maker's mark, the seller should provide a photo of the mark, too. (You can print out the photos.) You can e-mail the seller and ask for more photos or for close-ups of marks or damage. Not all sellers can provide extra photos, however.

How Will You Pay?

Be sure the auction listing includes information on how to pay the seller if you are the winning bidder (see "Payment Methods" below). *Remember: If you are the high bidder, you pay the seller, not the auction. Bidders, winning or not, are not charged anything by most online auctions.*

If the cost of shipping is not included, e-mail the seller and ask about it before you bid—because once you bid you have technically entered a legal contract. Shipping fees should cover all the costs of sending your item. This includes the cost of the box or bag, packing materials, postage, and fees for tracking and insurance. It may also include a fee for handling (the time involved in wrapping, boxing, taping, and labeling the package and taking it to the post office or shipper). Shipping fees are part of the cost of your purchase. The fees can be many dollars for large, heavy pieces. Consider shipping fees when you bid.

If the payment method and shipping charges are not mentioned in the listing, e-mail the seller. *If the seller does not answer your questions, DO NOT BID.*

Checking "Comments" (Feedback)

Most auction sites let bidders post comments about sellers and sales. When you're considering buying something, look at the comments posted about the seller to see what past buyers have said. Check the "feedback rating" probably found next to the seller's user name. Does the seller ship quickly? Does the seller handle problems calmly and reasonably?

If past buyers have made positive comments about a seller, but you're worried about a negative comment, e-mail the seller and ask what went wrong. If there are several comments from unhappy people, you probably should not buy from that seller.

All comments are permanent and public. Of course, mistakes do occur. The system is not infallible. As you become more experienced buying at Internet auctions, you will notice that regular sellers receive dozens of good comments and very few bad ones.

Automatic Bidding: A lot like absentee bidding at traditional auctions

You found what you want, and you're satisfied with the description, photos, and payment method. You're ready to bid. Many Internet auctions use what is called "automatic bidding," also called "proxy bidding." When you decide to bid on eBay, for instance, you enter the maximum amount you want to spend, click "review bid," and then click "agree to terms." Then eBay bids for you, a few dollars or cents at a time (the increments are determined by the current price), to maintain your bid as the highest, but keeps your maximum bid a secret. If bidding goes over your maximum, eBay stops bidding for you and sends you an e-mail telling you that you have been outbid. To continue competing for the item, you have to submit another maximum bid higher than the current high bid. (Refer to our chart at the end of the book, which reviews procedures for registering, bidding, and selling on the three largest online auctions: eBay, Amazon, and Yahoo.)

For example, if the high bid showing is $10, you can submit a bid of $15 knowing that eBay will enter your bid in the required increments, maybe 50 cents at a time, until it reaches your maximum bid of $15. If someone bids higher than your $15 maximum, you will receive an e-mail message from the auction telling you there is a higher bid than yours. If you wish, and there is time, you can place another, higher bid.

Check the auction regularly, every day if it just started, every hour the last day, and every few minutes, then seconds, near the end. That way, if you see the bid reach $16, you can bid again. Some bidders like to pop in a high bid ("snipe") at the last minute, jumping all the proxy bids (see "Sniping" under "Bidding Strategies," page 42), so you can never be sure your bid has won until the auction closes. Of course, if you submit an automatic maximum bid that's as high as you are willing to pay, all you care about is the final result. Automatic bidding produces less stress and takes up less time than sniping, although you may find you have less fun.

Most Internet auctions list the user names of the people bidding on the items being auctioned. The bidder's bids are kept secret until after the auction. You only know your own bid and the current high bid. Once you're an experienced bidder, you'll recognize some of the bidders' names and know which ones are regulars. If you have doubts about an item, and the regulars are not bidding, you may want to think again. On the other hand, some sellers don't know exactly what they're selling or may have spelled a word wrong in a listing, and many potential bidders may not find the item. If you are lucky, you may be the only buyer who spotted a good buy.

Reserve Prices: The same as traditional auctions

A "reserve" or "reserve price" is the lowest price a seller will accept for an item. The reserve price is not posted with the description. It's not included in the listing in a traditional auction catalog, either. The fact that there is a reserve is included on the auction Web page. Once the bidding starts, the auction tells you if the highest bid is below the reserve. So if the highest bid for a Royal Doulton figurine is $95 but the reserve is $100, the note will read: "$95, reserve not met." That means the $95 bidder won't get the figurine. Once the $100 reserve is met, the reserve note changes to read: "$110, reserve met." That means the figurine will sell for $110 or more. If the reserve is never met, the seller does not have to sell the Royal Doulton figurine to the highest bidder. Some sellers will tell you the reserve price during an ongoing auction. Others will not. E-mail and ask.

MAKE FRIENDS ON THE WEB

Track down others who share your collecting passion. You're likely to find myriad newsgroups, clubs, and individual collectors you can correspond with. They're good people to ask what auction sites or sellers to avoid and which ones are good. They can even alert you to auctions or sales you didn't know about.

Collectors Clubs

If you specialize in a collecting area, it is a good idea to join a collectors club whose members collect the same thing you do. For instance, if you collect Autumn Leaf dinnerware, you can join the National Autumn Leaf Collectors Club. Collectors clubs are a good source of information, including the latest news about fakes. If you have questions about something you want to buy online, you can contact another longtime club member for advice. If the club member is an expert and you have doubts about the authenticity or condition of the item you want to buy, he or she may be willing to take a look at the item online and offer you an educated opinion.

For a list of collectors clubs, see the book *Kovels' Yellow Pages,* or try searching for your collectible on the Internet. The club may have a Web site.

Bidding Strategies

DO-IT-YOURSELF BIDDING

You may choose not to depend on the automatic online bidding method. Instead, you can stay glued to your computer to see what happens during the auction. Brew a strong pot of coffee, because you may have to stay up late and bid continually if you want to win.

SNIPING

Some bidders like to wait and bid near the very end of an Internet auction's time-span, leapfrogging other bidders at the last minute—a practice called "sniping." The sniper is similar to the traditional-auction bidder who waits until the "going, going" to jump in with a bid just before the auctioneer says "gone."

Some bidders snipe because their user names are familiar to others who bid for the same type of collectible—so familiar that other collectors look at what these knowledgeable bidders are bidding on, then bid on the same thing—pushing prices up. Bidding during the last few seconds of an auction prevents this sort of "shadow shopping." Other bidders think sniping simply offers a better chance of winning an item.

Remember that although Internet auctions are worldwide, many run on Pacific Time. So if you live in another time zone, you have to adjust your thinking to Pacific Time when you check the ending time of an auction. If an auction ends at midnight Pacific Time, it's 3 A.M. in New York.

"COMPUTER GEEK" SNIPING

If you are a determined sniper and computer savvy, you can place bids faster if you open two Internet browsers at the same time. (While you are online, return to your desktop and click on your browser icon, or click on "Start" and "Programs" to find and open another copy of your browser.) On one browser window, keep the auction's bid form open and completed, so you can submit a new bid at a moment's notice. On the other browser window, follow the auction as it's going on. If possible, set it for "text only," so you don't waste time loading images you don't care about. Every few seconds, refresh the auction page (by clicking your "Refresh" button) so you can watch the bidding in real time. That way, you can jump over to the bid-form window quickly if you want to submit another bid. The speed of your Internet access, of course, affects the speed at which you can follow the auction and submit your bids.

Usually you start the process of sniping about five minutes before the auction closes. If you have not yet bid and really want the item, snipe with a bid that is the maximum amount you would want to pay—to win, you may have to bid as much as 50 percent higher than the current bid. Don't place a bid that's just one increment higher than the current high bid. You probably won't win. Fill in the bid form with your absolute maximum bid, get out your stopwatch, and submit your bid when there are only ten seconds left in the auction. By waiting that long, you increase your chances of winning.

The computer industry is constantly changing, and already there are software programs available that can snipe for you. If you hate the tension of sniping but like the results, you might want to buy one of these programs.

Auction Extension

Some online auctions, like many phone auctions, keep an auction going for five to thirty minutes after the last bid comes in. Others allow the seller to decide whether or not to allow an auction extension. If the auction is extended, you can click your "Refresh" button to see the new ending time. So if you snipe at the last minute in one of these auctions, the ending time automatically extends for a set time beyond the original closing time. You may have to keep sniping long after the original ending time.

Traditional phone auctions have used five-minute auction extensions for years, and live auctions do the same thing when the hammer is held until paddles stop going up.

KOVELS TIP!

Remember: If you are not the winning bidder but your high bid was close to the winner's, e-mail the seller and ask if she has more items like the one she just auctioned. If she does, she may sell one to you and avoid the cost and time involved in holding another auction. And don't be surprised if the seller, or some other person who sells the same type of collectible you bid on, contacts you to work out a private sale. Just don't pay more than you wanted to pay before you started bidding. You don't want to be lured into a buy you didn't want to make.

You Are the Successful Bidder

Each time you bid, you receive an e-mail from the auction site confirming your bid. The auction site will also e-mail you if you are outbid. If you are the successful bidder at the end of the auction, you receive an e-mail congratulating you at the same time the seller receives an e-mail from the auction telling her who won her auctioned item. (The auction site advises both you and the seller to e-mail each other to complete the sale.)

It's exciting to be the winning bidder at any auction. If you win an item online, you receive an "End of Auction" e-mail message from the auction telling you that you've won. (You receive an e-mail message saying "sorry" if you don't win.) Then the seller sends you an e-mail message to confirm the final price, including shipping and any other charges. The seller will tell you where to send your payment and how to pay. You e-mail the seller your address. It's a good idea to mail a completed self-addressed mailing label with your payment. That way, you can be sure the address on your package is correct. You should get the seller's phone number. Ask for it when you e-mail your address to the seller.

Payment Methods

Some sellers accept a personal check; others insist on a money order. NEVER SEND CASH. It's not safe, and provides no receipt, canceled check, or credit card statement that can serve as proof of payment. (U.S. postal and bank money orders, by the way, can be traced. Just save your receipt if you send a money order, and understand that tracing the money order can take considerable time.)

Some Internet auctions offer secure online payment services like PayPal (www.paypal.com) and Billpoint's Electronic Check (www.billpoint.com). Sellers decide whether or not they are willing to use these services. Sellers can also choose to take credit card payments using the same or similar online services. Secure servers allow buyers to send credit card, debit card, or bank account numbers over the Internet.

Amazon and eBay, among other online auctions, now provide a secure server to handle credit card or other electronic payments between their buyers and sellers, but not all sellers want to bother.

USE A SECURE BROWSER

The browser is the software used to navigate the World Wide Web. It should scramble purchase information—such as your credit card number—sent over the Web. When you are on the World Wide Web, you are using a browser like Microsoft Internet Explorer, Netscape, or AOL's browser. Newer versions of the browsers are more secure than older ones, and most Internet Service Providers (ISPs) and browsers let you know when a newer version is available for downloading. Currently, the most secure browsers available to the public use what is termed "128-bit encryption." An easy way to know if you're on a secure page is to look for a tiny yellow padlock icon on the bottom of your browser screen.

A secure server uses encryption to hide the numbers from Internet hackers. It is not foolproof, but it works well. Some sellers accept credit or debit card payments, but do not use a secure server. They will tell you to call with your credit card number (it is not safe to send your credit or debit card number via e-mail). Do not provide the seller with any other personal identifying numbers, such as your Social Security number, driver's license number, or bank account number.

Using a credit card gives you some recourse if what you bought is not what you expected. Read your credit card statement to learn the details about how to handle disputed charges. If you dispute a charge and have it taken off your credit card account, you have to immediately return the item to the seller. You pay all return shipping costs.

WARNING: Debit cards are handled as credit cards by sellers and secure servers, but they do not provide the same kind of protection as credit cards do. When your debit card charge reaches your bank, your money leaves your checking account—because using a debit card is the same as writing a personal check. You cannot dispute the charge the same way you can a charge on your credit card bill. Of course, you can go through legal channels to get your money back, but the process can take a long time and you are out the cash in the meantime. The same is true of electronic payments that automatically deduct money from your bank account.

If you and the seller agree to use an online payment method, whether it's a credit card, debit card, or another type of electronic

MODERN COMMEMORATIVE TINS

The modern commemorative tins often found at stores filled with candy or cookies have been garage-sale favorites for about ten years. Now collectors have organized. They have chat rooms and newsletters, and the sale of tins has moved to Internet auctions. Hundreds of tins are offered every day.

WARNING:
BUYER BEWARE OF FAKES

A few unscrupulous sellers deliberately offer fakes. Other sellers may offer fakes without knowing it. It can be particularly hard to deal with these unknowing sellers, because they believe they're selling genuine items. Fakes that have appeared on Internet auctions include "Vuitton" leather pieces, new pottery with old "Roseville" or "Nippon" marks, and new marbles that look like old ones. These fakes can't be spotted by looking at a photo.

A 1999 survey conducted by the *Wall Street Journal* found that half the antiques and collectibles listed on five Internet auction sites were misrepresented or described inaccurately. Always be very careful before you bid. The "buyer beware" rule is in force on the Internet.

payment, be sure to read the fine print when you sign up to use the payment method online. There may be limits on the amount of money that can be processed, and on the liability you, your bank, or the electronic payment service faces if there is a problem with the sale. Take advantage of the verification process some electronic payment services offer; it may take extra time for you to complete the necessary online forms, but it may protect you from fraud—whether you're the buyer or the seller.

Escrow Services

If you are buying an expensive item, both you and the seller may be more comfortable using an escrow service to hold your payment until you receive your purchase. Amazon and eBay offer an escrow service for a fee (usually 5 percent of the final sale price of the item). There are also other independent escrow services available online. The fee is usually paid by the buyer.

IF YOU DON'T WIN

"Selling out the back door" online. At a traditional auction, there is a little-known activity nicknamed "selling out the back door." When a piece, perhaps a Mission chair, doesn't meet its reserve, the consigner must take it back. But often the consigner really wants to get rid of the chair and tells the auction house after the auction that a lower price would be acceptable. The auction house will call some of the unsuccessful bidders and explain that the chair is available at a lower price. Or a collector may call the auction house and ask if the chair is now available for less.

If bids at an Internet auction do not reach the reserve price, there's a similar "out the back door" buying possibility. If you still want the Royal Doulton figurine and decided you will pay more than your highest registered bid, e-mail the seller and ask what the reserve was. The seller does not know what your maximum bid was. Let's say your highest recorded bid was $50 and your maximum bid was $75. Nobody won the figurine because even your $75 maximum did not meet the reserve price. You e-mail the seller and learn the reserve was $100. You might be able to negotiate a price you are willing to pay.

More on Returns

Sellers do not want you to return what you bought. Unless the item is not what was described when you bid (if you bid on a lunch box and got a toothbrush, for example), you are committed to the purchase. Sometimes, however, a seller will allow you to return an item if you explain your point of view (perhaps you dispute the "mint" condition of the vase you bought, because it has a big crack down the side). Your goal is to work out a return, but if a seller won't work with you, you can post negative feedback. Some sellers charge a "restocking fee" if you return an item.

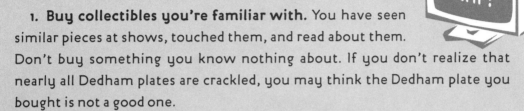

A FEW EXTRA BUYING TIPS FROM THE EXPERTS

1. **Buy collectibles you're familiar with.** You have seen similar pieces at shows, touched them, and read about them. Don't buy something you know nothing about. If you don't realize that nearly all Dedham plates are crackled, you may think the Dedham plate you bought is not a good one.

2. **Become familiar with your bidding competition.** Keep track of the user names of other bidders who are trying to buy the same kind of collectibles you want. It can be helpful. If a particular bidder always spends a lot more money than you want to spend, you can just avoid bidding against this bidder.

3. **Be careful if you're buying something expensive from an unfamiliar seller.** If you are seriously tempted, check the posted comments and ask other Internet collectors you know. If you're still worried, talk by phone with the seller. It's more revealing than e-mail. Just e-mail the seller and ask for a phone number.

4. **Federal regulations regarding fraud.** The Federal Trade Commission offers some protection against fraud. The FTC suggests that if you can safely use a credit card to buy (and the seller is willing to accept that form of payment), do it. You then have an extra layer of protection if the item is not what was promised. Again, never send cash.

5. **Damaged items.** If something arrives damaged, report it to the shipper and to the seller.

6. **Save e-mails.** Print and save copies of every e-mail exchanged between you and the seller. Keep them until you're sure the item is what you wanted.

7. **Take advantage of the extra fun possible.** Use the chat areas to "meet" other collectors.

Risks

There are risks to buying online, including fraud, disappointment with condition or quality, and breakage. Using an escrow system can help with the first two. Your money will not be given to the seller until you see and feel what you bought. If you're not happy, you return the item and get your money back from the escrow service. But you pay the escrow fee and return shipping.

Some online auctions now offer free insurance against fraud. If you pay for an item that costs less than $250 and it is never shipped to you, you can get your money back by filing a claim through the auction. Fraud is not a common occurrence, but there is certainly comfort in knowing that an auction offers financial protection against it. If you are buying something for more than $250, use an escrow service.

The best way to avoid the third problem, breakage, is to ask the seller to insure anything you buy, especially if it's fragile or valuable. Even furniture can be damaged in shipping. The seller can add the inexpensive cost of insurance to the shipping charge. Some sellers routinely insure everything they ship; others do not. So before you send your payment, ask the seller if his shipping fee includes insurance to cover the cost of the item you bought. If not, tell him to add the insurance cost to your bill.

Remind the seller to keep both the shipping and insurance receipts. You'll need them if you have to file a claim. If you receive your package and find that it was not insured, contact the seller and complain—and ask the seller to return the insurance fee to you. By the way, UPS shipments are routinely insured for $100. If what you bought cost less than that, the seller does not need to ask for additional insurance—or charge you an additional insurance fee.

Filing a Claim for a Broken Item

If your insured package arrives via U.S. mail and the contents are damaged, keep everything—broken pieces, damaged box, and labels. Some post offices reject claims if the contents of a package are destroyed but the package itself is not damaged. You must save the original package or your claim will be rejected. The claim itself has to be filed by the seller. You, the buyer, must go to the post office with the package and damaged contents. It is a time-consuming process.

United Parcel Service (UPS) and Federal Express (FedEx) also supply insurance, and claims for damaged packages are usually settled at your location. Again, keep all packaging and broken pieces until the claim is settled.

A SPECIAL NOTE ABOUT LIMITED EDITION COLLECTIBLES

KOVELS TIP!

If you collect "retired" (no longer produced) limited editions, whether dolls or plates or bells, you should be aware that online auctions sometimes serve as liquidation sites for retailers who are stuck with unsold limited editions from their shops. This may help you buy an old limited edition at a low price, but it also deflates the value of the collectible. The industry's "suggested retail value" for the collectible becomes irrelevant, because so many are selling online for 20 to 75 percent below their supposed values. Things that you once considered rare, and that may very well be rare in your area, can be found in multiples on the Internet. On the other hand, if more than one collector is seriously bidding on a limited edition, it could sell for more than the suggested retail value.

The benefit of e-commerce to a buyer and seller of retired limited edition collectibles is that matching buyer and seller is much easier than it used to be. A secondary market in these items is alive even if prices are not always predictable.

Fraud

Online auctions say that fraud is not a significant problem, but it can and does happen. The Federal Trade Commission reports that in 1999 it received more than 10,000 complaints about Internet auctions. Many of these complaints were not related to antiques or collectibles, but it is a worry nonetheless. Report problems at once. Online auctions will refuse business from sellers who have been caught selling forgeries or misrepresented items, or from those who have not delivered items for which they have been paid. In February 2000, eBay started forwarding all of its fraud complaints to the FTC's Consumer Sentinel fraud database. The FTC, in turn, has undertaken "Project Safebid," working with federal, state, and local law enforcement agencies to prosecute fraud cases. EBay has also formed a 200-person fraud team to work with users and law enforcement agencies.

TAKING PRECAUTIONS AGAINST FRAUD

There are intelligent precautions to take against fraud if you buy at online auctions:

1. Read the Help and FAQ (Frequently Asked Questions) pages on any auction site you are considering using. Some auction sites offer insurance against fraud (see page 56).

2. Explore the site for a while before you buy or sell.

3. Buy inexpensive items at first to help you get comfortable with the process and the auction site.

4. Buy a few items before you try selling—that way you get a feedback rating that makes selling easier for you.

5. When you're ready to buy, read the seller's feedback comments first.

6 Carefully read the seller's description of the item for sale, and then read it over again. Buyers sometimes complain about the descriptions sellers write, then realize later that the description was fair—they had just read it too fast to really understand it.

7 If the seller does not include a photo in the description, ask that a photo be sent to you via e-mail. Most online sellers can do this, even if they have to pay a photo service to scan it and send it to you.

8 If you have questions about the description, e-mail the seller. Ask the seller questions about condition, color, and marks that might be impossible to judge from the photo.

9 Ask about the exact cost of shipping—whether the seller charges what it costs to ship or if there is a handling fee added. If there is, is it reasonable or unfairly high?

10 Ask about the seller's return policy, especially if the item is expensive. Some sellers refuse to take returns, or charge a high "restocking fee." It is reasonable for the seller to charge a return fee that covers offering the item in another auction. The buyer always pays return shipping. There is only one reason for a return, and it is not "buyer's remorse." Return items only if you think the item you received is not what was described to you. (Reread the description—perhaps you expected more than the seller actually wrote.) Some buyers refuse to bid at auctions by sellers who say they will not take returns. Others insist on using an escrow service if the item is expensive. If you must return an item, contact the seller immediately and explain the situation. If he agrees to the return, ship the item at your expense within three days.

11　Use an escrow service if the item you want is expensive. Be sure before you buy that the seller is willing to do this. You pay the escrow fee.

12　Insist that the seller insure anything that's shipped to you, no matter what the price of the item, and no matter how unbreakable it is. Insurance covers loss as well as damage.

13　There are federal laws that govern mail, telephone, and Internet sales transactions. The seller must contact the buyer within 30 days, either by sending the merchandise, returning the check, or explaining the delay; otherwise charges can be filed against the seller. Fraud charges can be filed if the seller sold a fake. For detailed explanations of Federal Trade Commission regulations or to file a complaint, visit the FTC's Web site (www.ftc.gov). The FTC cannot resolve individual problems for consumers, but it can act against an individual or company if it sees "a pattern of possible law violations." You can also contact your state attorney general or your local consumer protection office if you have a serious concern.

DATE TRICKS

Just because a piece of glass is engraved 1905 or a plate has a mark on the bottom that includes the date 1766, don't conclude that the glass or plate is old. Fake souvenir ruby glass pieces with dates engraved on the side have been made since the 1950s. Many pottery marks include the date the factory was founded, not the date the piece was made. Do some research before you pay a high price online.

BOTTLE WARNING

Watch out for "enhanced" bottles offered for sale. Old bottles and telephone insulators are usually made of clear or pale aqua glass. A few rarities were made of colored glass and are expensive today. In the 1950s clear glass was put on a sunny rooftop in Arizona for a few years and the sun's ultraviolet rays turned the glass purple. Now artificial darkening is done quickly with modern machines. Dark purple, green, and brown glass bottles are being offered for sale. A common darkened bottle sells at flea markets for $10–$15, an insulator for $5. Dealers can buy them from the source for under $1. They are old but altered and are of value as decorations but not as historic glass. Don't overpay at any auction, on land or online. Read the description carefully. Ask if the color is recent.

Buyers Beware!

Nobody wants to get taken, especially when buying on the Internet. Returning merchandise to—or getting a refund from—an unfamiliar seller may be difficult, or impossible. There are steps to take that can protect you from making costly mistakes:

GET TO KNOW THE SELLER. Never do business with an anonymous user. Most sites offer user profiles, so you can learn the real names of sellers and buyers, and most sites also post comments others have made about sellers and buyers. Be suspicious, though. Sellers could plant their own positive comments. (Sellers can check, too, to see if a buyer is known for paying on time.) Get the seller's phone number and mailing address. Don't settle for only a P.O. box—a favorite of fly-by-nights. The seller may prefer that you send your payment to a post office box, but insist on getting the seller's street address as well. If you're still worried, contact the Better Business Bureau or a consumer protection agency for any information they may have on the seller.

KNOW WHAT YOU'RE BUYING. This is not the time to branch out into buying items with which you are unfamiliar. Be sure to read the description carefully. Be wary of descriptions of collectibles. If the seller uses unprofessional terms that a serious collector would not use to describe condition (such as "very nice" when talking about a baseball card), he could be trying to pass off a below-grade item. If a seller fails to mention condition at all, use *extreme* caution. Misspellings in the description might mean someone is trying to pass off a fake or is unfamiliar with collecting. Do your research before you bid. Have a good idea of what you should be paying. Check in a price book like *Kovels' Antiques & Collectibles Price List* or an online price site like www.kovels.com.

CHECK OUT THE SITE'S INSURANCE. Some auction sites offer insurance against bad deals when you don't get what you ordered, or don't get anything at all. Find out how much the site insurance will pay. If the auction site offers no insurance or less than you need, consider an *escrow service,* which holds your money until you receive and approve the merchandise. There will be a fee, usually based on the item's cost. Our list of helpful Web sites at the end of the book includes escrow services.

WHEN YOU'RE READY TO BID. Ask about delivery and returns. Know before you bid who will pay shipping (and what the shipping will cost) and what kind of return policy the seller has. Document everything related to the transaction—print and keep the auction listing, e-mails, cancelled checks, credit card receipts, phone bills, and faxes. This information could be vital to any claim you might have to make. **Don't give out your Social**

Security, driver's license, or bank account numbers when bidding—or to anyone online. None of these numbers have to be used to verify your identity. Always pay by credit card when you can. Federal law says credit card users have the right to dispute charges for goods they don't receive or that aren't what they ordered. If there's a problem, though, report it within 60 days of the charge's appearance on your credit card statement. The credit card company will investigate your claim.

A CHANGING BUSINESS

Dealers we see at shows tell of various experiences buying or selling using eBay, Amazon, Yahoo, and other online auctions. A Michigan dealer said she liked to interact with real people, so online auctions did not interest her. An Ohio dealer with high-priced leather items said he had very bad luck buying online because most of the pieces he looked at were incorrectly described—the "alligator" purse was really pressed leather, and the "leopard" jacket was stenciled rabbit. But a Florida dealer said he sells thousands of dollars' worth of bronzes a month online, more than he sells in his shop. The bronzes are expensive, so he uses an escrow service for his online sales.

We hear both collectors and dealers moan about how the business is changing and how shops and shows could disappear. Relax. Nothing can replace impulse buying at a shop. Looking, feeling, and touching collectibles and talking to dealers are part of the fun. An afternoon of "antiquing" will never be totally replaced by a lonely session at a computer keyboard. However, as a result of online auctions, there probably will be fewer shops and shows and a rethinking of how to advertise and display collectibles to bring in buyers. Shows are already becoming more specialized, focusing on a single area of collecting (such as toys or Depression glass), and malls are springing up in all parts of the country. The good news is that the antiques and collectibles business is getting bigger while it's changing.

IF YOU'RE CHEATED. When the Fenton glass lamp arrives and is obviously a fake, first contact the seller. Give him a triple whammy of e-mail, phone call, and snail mail (regular mail). Be nice. Perhaps there was a mistake or misunderstanding; perhaps the seller didn't know the lamp was a fake. If that doesn't work, see if the site offers a dispute resolution service. SquareTrade (www.squaretrade.com) provides a mediator to resolve such disputes. It's free to file a case on the site and to use the site's system to respond to each other as you try to work out an agreement. (If the problem arose over an eBay transaction, the value of the item has to be at least $100 and the transaction date within the last 30 days.) If you want SquareTrade to mediate your dispute, you will be charged $15 if the transaction was done on eBay, or $10 plus 2.5 percent of the amount in question if the transaction occurred on another site. If dispute resolution isn't available, practical, or desirable, contact your local district attorney, state attorney general, the auction site, and the Better Business Bureau.

WARN OTHERS! If you've been had, post negative feedback in the seller's file. (Don't get emotional—just the facts, ma'am.) Also, the Federal Trade Commission's Consumer Response Center can act against a company if it sees a pattern of violations —let them know what happened to you (877-382-4357 or www.ftc.gov/ftc/complaint.htm). The Internet Fraud Complaint Center reviews complaints and may refer them to law enforcement or regulatory agencies (www.ifccfbi.gov). The National Consumers League's National Fraud Information Center will want to know (www.fraud.org). Fraud.org reports receiving 1,500 e-mails and 120,000 visits each week—this is a site you may want to check out before you bid!

Cyber-Shills

Shill bidding—when the seller, or more likely a friend, enters fake bids to drive up prices—doesn't happen only in the real world. It can happen on the Internet, too. Shill bidding falls under the heading of auction fraud and should be reported to the authorities. Some auction sites use shill software to protect their buyers. The software keeps track of the bidding history of the auction site's users. It may take them awhile, though, to figure things out. Perhaps you will notice a pattern of bidding on your own.

A Few More Words of Warning

CHARITY SCAMS. Charity scams are plentiful. Don't be fooled by sellers who claim to be auctioning items for charity. The tip-off is that the name of the charity isn't specified or is unfamiliar.

DON'T BUY FROM POST-AUCTION E-MAILS. After you've bid on an item and lost it, the seller may e-mail you and offer to sell you similar items. The seller may have been using the auction to lure you.

ONLINE AUCTION RULES FOR BUYERS

1. Ask the seller your questions early in the auction so you're not surprised later.
2. Once you win an item, respond quickly to the seller's e-mail.
3. Follow the seller's shipping and payment terms, even if you would have preferred different methods.
4. Send your payment promptly, and e-mail the seller to tell him exactly when you mailed your payment.
5. E-mail the seller as soon as you receive the item.
6. If a problem arises, e-mail the seller and try to agree on a solution to the problem.
7. Post positive feedback about the seller if you're satisfied. It's the nice thing to do.

A Buyer's Diary

MONDAY

1:17 P.M.   Doris's birthday is next week. She makes delicious deviled eggs and is known for her collection of egg plates. Maybe I can find one on eBay.

1:20   Search "egg plates"; 190 auctions come up.

1:21   Find one I like, green pottery by Lefton, very attractive.

1:22   Enter a bid, receive error message "the page cannot be displayed"; obviously eBay is having a bad day! Log off and on again to see if it will help.

1:30   Manage to get in bid. Current price was $15, decide to enter $25 proxy bid (will bid again up to $30 if need be). Bid accepted, current price now up to $15.50. Auction ends around 7:30 this evening, my time.

6:40   Log on to check the auction; discover I was outbid this afternoon. Price now up to $25.50 ($.50 over my proxy bid). Decide to up my bid to $29.79.

6:45   Log off for son's phone call, but leave browser window open to auction page for easy access.

7:00   Log on again, hit "Refresh" button to update auction page—still winning! Will stay on.

7:03	Walk away to make Kool-Aid for son, come back and hit "Refresh" button again. Still winning.
7:05	Have 10 minutes to kill; decide to scope out the competition. Click on "Bid History" link and copy other bidder's ID with my mouse, then use "Back" key to return to auction page. Hit "Refresh" to see current bid; still winning. Open second browser window, go to eBay's search page and paste user's name into the "Find items by bidder" window.
7:08	Yikes! The other bidder collects egg plates; better be prepared to snipe! Return to first browser window with auction page.
7:12	Open auction page on second browser and prepare to enter higher bid, hitting "Refresh" on first browser window every minute or so.
7:14	Start hitting "Refresh" every 10 seconds.
7:17:29	Whew, no need to snipe, I have the winning bid! Might as well dash off a note to the seller now.
7:21	Send e-mail with cordial greeting, name, and address to seller. Will wait for reply.
11:00	Log on to check e-mail one more time before bed. Receive e-mail with shipping amount from seller.

11:03	Send reply e-mail.

TUESDAY

5:05 P.M.	Arrive at post office to buy money order, find out the branch closed at 5:00 (some are open until 5:30). Oh, shucks. Prefer postal money order, so I'll go again next morning.

WEDNESDAY

8:30 A.M.	Leave home to stop at post office before work.
8:40	Long line, finally have money order; total is $32.64 ($26.50 for item, $5.00 for shipping—including $.85 for insurance—$.80 for money order, $.34 for postage).
8:45	I carefully fill out information on money order. The fine print on back of money order states: "This receipt is your guarantee for a refund of your money order if it is lost or stolen, provided you fill in the PAY TO and FROM information on the money order in the space provided." This is why I always use a postal money order. I take the time to fill it out completely and file the tear-off receipt with printouts of the auction page and pertinent e-mails.
8:50	Payment goes into the mail slot. Off to work. Hope my payment gets there quickly and the seller ships the package immediately.

Following WEDNESDAY

11:00 A.M. Receive the package! It was sent by Priority Mail on Monday. It's cutting it close, but the egg plate is here in time for my friend's birthday. Whew!

11:15 Finally make it through all the layers of the package—egg plate is beautiful. The color is not as dark as the photo and there's a tiny white mark on the front where the glaze is missing. The flaw wasn't described in the auction listing, and the photo is no longer online, so I can't check to see if it showed up there. Oh well, it's not too noticeable. I turn the plate over and notice a couple more unglazed spots. The seller really should have stated this. She called the plate "mint." I'll have to be more careful next time. I don't know if I'll give it to my friend as a gift because the flaws are too noticeable.

11:45 Send e-mail to seller saying I received the plate. I thank her for the speedy delivery and smooth transaction. I decide not to bring up the flaws—they aren't really damage. They're probably stilt marks from the firing process.

12:30 P.M. Pull out the egg plate again to look closely at the mark. It's not stamped on or under the glaze. There's a clear plastic label with the words "Lefton China Handpainted" and the crown logo in black. I wonder if this is really a Lefton plate.

2:00   This is beginning to bother me. Too bad I already sent the e-mail to the seller. How can I find out if this is really a Lefton item? Was I taken?

2:15   I look at my book on Lefton china. The egg plate isn't listed. The mark isn't like any in the book. I'm trying to stay calm.

3:00   I make a call to a friend who collects Lefton. She has old catalogs from twenty years ago. Maybe she can help.

4:00   My friend is at home and willing to let me look through her catalogs. Sure enough, I find my egg plate in a 1979 catalog. Whew. It's also in the 1982 and 1985 catalogs, so it was made for a while.

7:00   Much calmer now, but I've learned a lesson. Next time I'll look up the item before I bid. I'm not an avid Lefton collector, so I could have really been burned. I shouldn't have placed my bid in such a hurry.

Selling on
the Internet

Who Sells on the Internet?

Some online sellers use an Internet auction the way they would use a garage sale. It's a place to sell stuff they no longer want. Others are pros, and use Internet auction sites as routes to make money for either a home-based business or for a shop that can reach additional customers online. The Internet is particularly profitable for dealers in rare books, maps, World's Fair souvenirs, photographs, postcards, royalty items, obscure patterns of dishes and silverware, and other collectibles that are hard to find and small enough to ship easily.

Many dealers hire specialists to photograph and list items for Internet auctions. Some dealers, even those with traditional shops, open online shops on Internet malls like The Internet Antique Shop (TIAS, at www.tias.com) or Ruby Lane (www.rubylane.com). These Internet malls may or may not charge dealers to put their shops online. Internet malls give dealers a convenient and high-profile way to sell over the Internet, and also offer a link to online auctions. For example, a dealer who tried selling a Royal Doulton jug in her shop can offer it at her shop site on the Internet mall. If it still doesn't sell, she can click on her mouse and tell the mall to send the jug to an online auction site.

But most online auction sellers are not professional dealers. They are collectors who want to buy and sell through the large national and international market now available over the Internet.

Preparing to Sell Online

If you want to sell an antique or collectible online, you have to make a few decisions. Is your item, let's say a green pottery bowl, a fairly common item? A rare and exceptionally beautiful piece? Or don't you know? Is it marked? Was it made by an important artist or factory? Is it in perfect condition? No matter how you answer these questions, selling online may be a good option.

If your bowl is common, you'll probably get the going price for it online—but will selling online be worth the time it takes you to type in the description, post a photo, handle a long-distance payment, and ship the bowl packed so it won't break? After all, you could easily sell your bowl at a local shop, show, or mall. But if you want to try an online auction without risking much, go ahead and auction your bowl. Once you've sold your first item via an online auction, the process becomes smoother.

If you have a rare item with an identifiable pattern, mark, or maker, perhaps a piece of Ohr pottery, it could bring a surprisingly good price on the Internet because it will be seen by so many potential buyers.

If you are not sure of the value of your bowl, the Internet presents a unique opportunity. Your bowl will be seen by a very large group of people, and some of them will know more about what you have than you do—and may bid high for it.

Choosing an Auction Site

If you want to sell your green pottery bowl online, use an Internet auction site that lists a lot of pottery. That is where you will find buyers for your bowl. The same rule is true no matter what you're selling. If you want to sell an animated clock, use an auction that offers a lot of clocks.

How to List Your Item at Auction

CREATING A TITLE: YOUR ONLINE AD

You have to write a title and description for your item before you even go online. This is much like writing a classified ad for a

EIGHT TOUGH THINGS TO SELL ON THE INTERNET AND WHY

1. **Very large pieces of furniture**. They're too hard to ship and expensive to return, so buyers are wary. Hope for a customer who lives nearby.

2. **Clear glass with no marks.** It does not photograph well and can't be identified easily by the buyer. Chips and flaws do not show in photos.

3. **Diamonds and diamond jewelry.** After delivery, the buyer could switch large stones and then claim the seller misrepresented the item. Diamond grading takes an expert and requires certified appraisals.

4. **Autographed sports memorabilia.** Forgeries abound and are well publicized. Smart buyers won't buy from an unfamiliar seller.

5. **The Congressional Medal of Honor, an Oscar, the Heisman Trophy,** or other awards that may not clearly belong to the buyer or seller. They could be confiscated by the original organization that awarded the medal or trophy.

6. **Damaged merchandise.** Buyers want to buy items in perfect (or close) condition.

7. **Anything that you sold last week**. Buyers like "fresh" merchandise and will ignore a repeat offer.

8. **Marbles.** The fakes from Mexico are so good they look authentic in a picture. Knowledgeable buyers who might spend $300 for a real marble know that fakes are being made and they won't bid on a marble from an unknown seller. The Superman marble (with blue-and red-colored swirls) sells for over $300 if real, but costs less than $10 if fake.

newspaper. Let's say you want to sell a Dedham pottery plate. Think about how your ad will appeal to potential buyers. Create a title for your plate using a limited number of letters and spaces (each letter and space between words counts as one "character"). The auction's software sets the limit—usually 45 characters or less—and the words in the title will be the ones that will lead online shoppers to your plate.

When you choose your title, think about collectors who might want to buy your plate. How would they describe what they're looking for? If your Dedham plate is in mint condition and has a rabbit design around the border, you could title it: "Dedham pottery rabbit plate, mint." That's 33 characters, counting spaces. You've entered all the important "search" words (Dedham, pottery, rabbit, plate) and the important descriptive word (mint).

TEN EXAMPLES OF GOOD TITLES

Adam Depression glass sugar, creamer, green

Tammis Keefe hanky/hankie, brown, w/flowers

Art deco style Telechron blue mirror clock

Vintage 1960s metal wire black phone stand

Victorian art glass Burmese vase, flowers

Fiesta 15 in. red chop plate, round platter

Claire McCardell black&white checked gloves

Space age orange Italy espresso pot Eames era

Ornate Victorian brocade footstool/foot stool

Retro Mirro cookie & pastry press w/box

Most auction sites limit the number of characters and spaces you can use to identify your auction item. On eBay, the "Sell" form accepts only 45 characters. The examples above make use of the limited space by including only factual words that describe the item.

Wasting space with subjective words like "beautiful," "wonderful," or "really cute" doesn't help potential bidders find your item. Who would use the word "cute" to search for her favorite salt and pepper shakers? A bidder would look for a color, pattern name, manufacturer, or designer.

Sometimes it's necessary to second-guess potential bidders. Will a bidder look for a "hanky" or "hankie," a "footstool" or "foot stool"? By including both forms, you have covered your bases.

The "/" (slash) is ignored by most search engines, so you can use "w/" to abbreviate "with" and save two characters and one space. The "&" (ampersand) is also ignored, so you can save two spaces by typing "black&white" in your title.

When it's difficult to pin an age or style on your item, use terms like Space Age, or Art Deco style. There are many users who look for these terms specifically. See "Decoding Collectible Jargon" on page 72.

THE DESCRIPTION

Once potential buyers find your title, they can read your lengthier description to learn more. Be complete and be truthful. There is usually no limit on space for your description, but you should keep it under 500 words. Remember, you must include size, color, name of maker, pattern, mark, and dates. Whatever you know. Don't let your creativity lie dormant. Draw a picture with your words. If you are selling a vase with a yellow base and dripping white glaze, you can call it a "mustard-colored vase, with thick, glossy, white drip glaze."

You also must include condition in the description. Go into detail, describing any problem honestly. Collectors expect to see one of these terms in your description of condition: mint, nearmint, excellent, very good, good, or fair. If it's in poor condition, don't bother trying to sell it. Use your best judgment, and

be fair. Remember, "mint" means absolutely perfect, no nicks, scratches, or even glaze flaws. A "mint" item is in unused, new condition. No vase with a crack or chip is in better than fair condition.

DECODING COLLECTIBLE JARGON

AOP: Allover pattern.

C & S: Cup and saucer.

DG: Depression glass.

EAMES ERA: Broadly used to refer to home accessories that resemble Ray and Charles Eames' modern designs. Items date from the 1940s to 1970s.

EAPG: Early American pressed glass.

NR: No reserve.

MIB: Mint in box. Refers to an item in perfect condition and in its original box.

MIE: Made in England.

MOP: Mother-of-pearl.

MINT: Absolutely perfect and probably never used. There are no discolorations, scratches, or manufacturing flaws. Be very careful when using this term. Mint is better than excellent.

PUG: Painted under glaze; often used to refer to steins.

RETRO: Anything more than 20–25 years old, often with a whimsical or nostalgic quality. For jewelry, it means 1940s design.

S & P: Salt and pepper.

SASE: Self-addressed stamped envelope.

SHABBY CHIC: Refers to a decorating style. Items are usually home accessories with flowers, soft textures, and pastel colors that date from the 1940s or 1950s.

SPACE AGE: Refers to ultramodern designs of the 1960s and 1970s. Items are usually plastic or metal with chrome accents and bright colors.

VINTAGE: An evolving definition; usually refers to anything more than 20–25 years old.

TYPING YOUR DESCRIPTION

You can type your description using your word-processing program or Windows Notepad. That way, you won't be wasting time online crafting your words. When you are finished writing your description, "copy" it, then go online and "paste" what you wrote into the description box when you list your item for sale. Copying and pasting involve moving your mouse cursor over the description you wrote so it's highlighted, clicking "Edit" on the toolbar at the top of your screen, then clicking on the word "Copy." Now go online, and when you're ready to insert the description you wrote, click "Edit" again, then "Paste."

BE SURE TO SPELL WORDS CORRECTLY. If you misspell words, your potential buyers won't find your item—because the auction's search engine won't find what you're selling. Some smart buyers look for misspelled words like "Wedgewood" instead of Wedgwood or "Limoge" instead of Limoges. That's because savvy buyers know that fewer bidders will find the misspelled items, and that a bargain may be available. Some sellers include both spellings in a title ("hanky" and "hankie," for example) so that shoppers will find the listing with either spelling. (See "Spell Chek" on page 34.)

Correct spelling and grammar are important for another reason. They affect your image. If you appear careless and unintelligent, buyers will doubt your description.

Use the singular form of a word, not the plural, when you type your title. Some search engines make a distinction, and sellers and buyers tend to use the singular. Most search engines don't distinguish between capital and small (upper and lower case) letters. Your listing for a Depression glass bowl will be found whether you type "Depression" or "depression."

LEARN A LITTLE HTML. Most auctions allow you to use this special Web computer language in your description. It's easy to learn the basics, and the result is a more spirited, attractive description. (See our explanation of basic HTML code, below.)

MONEY-BACK GUARANTEE? More and more sellers are including a note in the description offering a money-back guarantee. This reassures bidders that your item is authentic and that if they win the item, they'll have no trouble returning it if they're not 100-percent pleased.

MAKE YOUR DESCRIPTION STAND OUT

Improve the appearance of the text in your auction description by using a few basic HTML (hypertext markup language) codes. The codes go in front and at the end of the word or phrase you want to embellish. There are more codes you can use to add graphics, photos, lists, or tables. You can learn more about HTML in books like *HTML for Dummies*, by Ed Tittel. There are also online references like the Web site "Marshall Brain's How Stuff Works" (www.howstuffworks.com). See our list of "Image Hosts, Counters, Batch Loaders & Other Auction Services" at the end of this book for sites that offer programs that put the HTML codes in place for you.

HTML CODE	RESULT
<b></b>	**bold type**
<i> </i>	*italics*
<u> </u>	<u>underlined type</u>
<small>	type is one size smaller
<big> </big>	type is one size bigger
<center></center>	type is centered
<font color=red> </font>	red type (font color code allows choice of colors)
 	breaks the line
<hr>	makes a horizontal line

Here's a sample description with HTML codes in place:

```
<center><b><big>Great Find!</big></b></center>
<br>
```
I found this wonderful McCormick & Co. cookbook in my mother's attic. The cover says `<b>Selected Recipes That Keep the Family Happy</b>`. The copyright date is 1928 and the cookbook measures 8 x 5 in. There is `<u>minor</u>` damage to the upper right corner.`<br>`
`<br>`
Successful bidder must pay by money order and include $3.50 for Priority Mail shipping.
`<hr>`
`<small>`Please, `<font color=red>`serious bidders only! `</font>` I will leave negative feedback if you back out of this sale.`</small>`

The description would look like this online:

GREAT FIND!

I found this wonderful McCormick & Co.
cookbook in my mother's attic. The cover says
Selected Recipes That Keep the Family Happy.
The copyright date is 1928 and the cookbook measures 8 x 5 in.
There is <u>minor</u> damage to the upper right corner.

Successful bidder must pay by money order
and include $3.50 for Priority Mail shipping.

Please, serious bidders only!
I will leave negative feedback if you back out of this sale.

WHAT TO INCLUDE IN YOUR DESCRIPTION

Brand name, maker, or manufacturer. Many people search by these names.

Artist or designer. Go ahead and boast that you have a Tiffany. It'll pay off.

Date the item was made. Look for obvious dates, or date by patent mark, or give a general description, such as "Depression era."

Country of origin. Some collectors look for items from certain countries, so include this information if you know it.

Medium or material. People will want to know if your table is oak or maple and if your book is leather-bound or not.

Maker's marks and model numbers. Do include any artist's signature or manufacturer's mark. Even if it doesn't mean anything to you, a collector will be able to gain information from it. The model number on items like radios or toys is also important.

Color and size. The color may not show up accurately on the photo. Size is especially important if the item is large—people have to know if it will fit in their house.

Reserve status. Don't care what you get for Aunt Vickie's embroidered tablecloth? Set a "No Reserve" status and let the buyers go wild. If you've got an investment in something you can't afford to lose at a bargain, set a reserve at the lowest price you could accept.

Bad Description vs. Good Description

BAD

Title: Beautiful Egg Plate

First bid: $7.00

Description: This is an egg and relish dish. It will hold 12 eggs. The width is 10". A nice addition to your holiday table. Buyer pays S&H. Money order next day mail, personal check 10 days. Thanks for looking.
(Included two photos of clear glass egg plate)

GOOD

Title: Fire-King Turquoise Blue Egg Plate No Res.

First bid: $8.99

Description: This great piece is in near mint condition . . . Not alot of the 22K gold has worn off. It, of course, has been used . . . Please add $4.50 s/h plus insurance. Allow 7–10 days for personal checks to clear. Money orders/cashiers checks/PayPal shipped NEXT DAY!! Will ship to Alaska, Hawaii and Canada for actual shipping and insurance fees. Any questions please don't hesitate to e-mail me. Check out my other auctions. Multiple orders means less shipping fees!! PayPal means you see this in your hands faster!! MS residents add 7% sales tax. Thank you for looking and GOOD LUCK!!
(Included two photos, front and back of egg plate)

Both of these descriptions are reprinted word-for-word as they appeared online. The first egg plate didn't sell (according to the "hits counter" added by the seller, only one user looked at the page). The second egg plate had a bidder within 24 hours of posting. It sold for $16.27 with a total of seven bids by four bidders.

Why?

The first egg plate lacks any real description in the title. Sure, it comes up if you're searching for "egg plate," but what if you searched for "glass egg plate"? It would have been overlooked.

KOVELS TIP!

THE DOS AND DON'TS OF AUCTION DESCRIPTIONS

DO include the amount of postage and shipping charges. People are reluctant to bid when they don't know what the postage costs will add to the final bid.

DO describe your item fully and accurately. Include scratches, nicks, or faded spots. The buyer will know what she's getting and you'll be less likely to be saddled with returns from unhappy buyers.

DO include documentation and provenance. If the twin or cousin of your item appears in one of our books, for instance, include that in the description. Potential buyers can see what they're getting. And if you can document the ownership history of your treasure to a celebrity or an expert in the field, by all means do it!

DON'T include huge picture files that take a long time to load. Not everyone has a super-duper computer and fast cable modem that can handle it.

DON'T include music and blinking words! They are distracting.

DON'T use clichés. Overblown descriptions that include phrases like "one of a kind," "unique," "rare," or "a great addition to your collection" turn off serious collectors.

The description included a photo, which revealed it is a clear Fire-King glass egg plate. With additional description, the egg plate might have attracted glass collectors in general and Fire-King collectors specifically. The second egg plate stated the color and the maker in its description, making it searchable to bidders with specific tastes.

Other factors that made the second plate more attractive to bidders were the statement about the condition of the plate and the details about shipping and handling. Bidders are more confident about a purchase if they don't have to worry about exorbitant shipping costs or whether the item has flaws that aren't easily seen in the photo.

Minimum Bids

Most Internet auctions require you to set a "minimum bid" for the item you are selling. The minimum bid is the price at which bidding for your item will start. No bid lower than that will be taken. Some auctions, like eBay and Amazon, charge a listing fee that's figured by the price you set as your minimum bid. The lower your minimum bid, the lower your listing fee. There's another reason not to set a high minimum: High minimum bids could discourage potential bidders. If you set your minimum bid at the current market value, bidders will stay away, figuring they will probably wind up paying too much for what you're selling. If you are concerned about selling at too low a price, set a reserve price.

Reserve Prices

A "reserve" or "reserve price" is the lowest price at which you will sell your item. The reserve you set for your vase or bowl or baseball card is usually not the same amount you set as your minimum bid. Auctions do not require you to set a reserve price. But you can set a reserve to be sure you don't have to sell your bowl for too little. Just remember, too high a reserve may mean your piece won't sell at all. And you will still owe the auction a "reserve fee" because you set a reserve price.

How to Include a Photograph with Your Listing

Pictures help you get higher prices online. A couple of years ago, few sellers posted photos. Today, with inexpensive scanners and digital cameras available, most sellers do. In fact, it is not easy to sell today without a photo. There are several methods you can use to post a photo, and none of them are simple. But if you are patient and have the right computer software and hardware, you can do it. And after you have done it once or twice, it will be easy.

↗ Take a good, focused photograph of your bowl. Get close enough so that the bowl is as large as possible (but focused) in the photo. Also take a close-up photo of the mark. You can use any kind of camera. Digital cameras store photos on an internal disk that can be directly accessed by your computer if you have the right software. If you have a standard camera, you can ask the developer to save the photos as .jpg files (JPEG format) on a CD-ROM or floppy disk, or you can get the photos developed on paper the traditional way. If you have traditional photographs, you can use your scanner and photo software to create .jpg files on your computer.

↗ Once your computer has stored your photo as a .jpg file, you have to link the photo to the description of your item. You do this by creating a URL (uniform resource locator) for your photo. There are three basic ways to do this. You can:

1 Create your own Web site.

2 Use a service offered by your ISP (Internet Service Provider).

3 Use an "image-hosting" Web site like www.
auctionwatch.com or www.picturebay.com.

↗ Once you have a URL for your photo, you simply type the
URL's address into the appropriate box on the same screen
where you type your description.

↗ If you have trouble with any of these steps, read the tutorials
available at the auction site or at the photo-handling Web site.
These tutorials give you detailed steps and suggestions. They
tell you what size photo to use, what resolution to use, what
equipment you need, and who you can contact for help.

Selling on a Large Auction Web Site Like eBay or Amazon

*You have drafted a title and description of, for instance,
your green pottery bowl. You have also taken photos and
set your price. It is time to actually sell on the auction
Web site. We'll use eBay as an example here. Refer to our
chart at the end of the book comparing eBay, Amazon,
and Yahoo for more detailed information on the three
most popular online auction sites.*

Open eBay's Web site (www.ebay.com) and click on the icon
that asks you to register as an eBay user. Only registered users can
list items for sale. If you already registered to buy items, you do
not have to register again to sell. If you did not register before, do
it now. We explain registration procedures in Part II of this book.

Now follow the necessary steps outlined on eBay's "Sell" page.
Fill out the registration form on the screen. First type in the title
you decided to give your bowl, using up to 45 letters and spaces.
You cannot include asterisks or quotation marks. Then choose
the category (your choices include Antiques & Art, Collectibles,

Dolls, Figures, Pottery & Glass, and Toys) and subcategories (also listed) under which you will list your item.

Think carefully when you choose a category and subcategories. Some items may fit under a few different headings. A pottery bowl, for instance, would most likely be listed in the Pottery & Glass category, but it might also be found in the Collectibles category under the subcategory Kitchenware. Within the Collectibles category, a cast-iron advertising ashtray could be listed in various subcategories, such as Advertising, General; Metalware, Cast Iron; or Tobacciana, Ashtrays. Many collectors looking for your ashtray will do a search rather than browse the Web site's subcategories, so your ashtray will be found no matter which subcategory you choose. But to take the most advantage of the site, check to see where most advertising ashtrays are listed and use the same subcategory.

The next section of the form is a box for the description of your item. Type a full description of your green pottery bowl. Include dimensions, colors, marks, condition including repairs and parts that are not original, and whether or not you have the original box. It is helpful to include how and where you obtained the item: "from an old Ohio grocery store closed since 1940" or "bought at the 1939 World's Fair by my grandmother."

Next, enter the URL where a photo of your bowl is posted on the Internet. (See "How to Include a Photograph with Your Listing," pages 80–81.) Then decide if you want some of the extra advertising services offered, such as bold type for your title or listing as a "Featured" item. You pay for these extras. They range in price from 25 cents to $100.

Finally, the registration form asks for your location (city and state if you're in the United States); the payment methods you will accept (COD, money order, personal check, certified bank check, credit or debit card, or one of the newer forms of electronic payment methods, such as Billpoint's Electronic Check); whether you will accept an escrow payment; where you will ship (nationally or internationally); your shipping charge and whether

home | my eBay | site map | sign in

eBay™

| Browse | Sell | Services | Search | Help | Community |

sell your item form

half.com an eBay company
Special eBay offer: Save $5 on a $10 order!

[ ] **Search**

Smart Search

☐ Search titles **and** descriptions

Sell Your Item

Related Links: • New to Selling?   • Seller Tips   • Fees   • Registration
• Free Shipping Estimates from iShip.com

Before you can sell...
1) You must be a registered eBay user.
2) You must provide a valid credit card if you are new to selling. Why?
3) Make sure your item is allowed on eBay.

Attention all eBay sellers!

▶Starting on October 9th, ALL sellers who have not selected their photo hosting preference will access a new, one-time photo hosting preference page, where they will need to select their photo hosting service. We will use a cookie to remember your preference so you do not have to see this page again after you have made your decision. Learn more.
▶ NEW! eBay's photo hosting service lets you add two pictures per listing for **FREE**.
If you use Internet Explorer 4.0+, a 1-time 1-step ActiveX download is required.
For all other browsers - no download is required!

First, choose a Main Category:
(you'll choose a subcategory on the next page)

Why did this page change?

You can still choose from all the categories at once by clicking here.

Antiques & Art
Fine art, glass, ceramics, furniture, and more.
NEW! Free counters now available in this category

Automotive--eBay Motors
Used cars, collector cars, motorcycles, and related parts and accessories.

eBay Motors. Click Here

Jewelry, Gemstones
Antique, comtemporary, watches, artist, and beads

Photo & Electronics
Audio, electronics, and photo and video equipment

Pottery & Glass
China, porcelain, and stoneware

Real Estate
Residential, land, commercial, and more...

When you click "Sell" on the eBay home page, you reach the screen above. If you are already registered, you can pick your category and start listing your item for sale. If you have not registered, you must do so now.
You have to register to sell or buy on eBay, and you have to provide credit card information if you want to sell. To register from this page, click on the word "Registration" to the right of the words "Sell Your Item."

you or the buyer pays shipping; your minimum bid; your user name and password; and your own credit card information (so the auction can bill you for its fees). You also choose a length of time your auction will last (most last seven days, but you can shorten yours to three days or expand it to ten).

Once you complete the form, press the "Review" button at the bottom, then "Place" your listing. Within a short time, eBay sends you an e-mail confirmation of your listing, including a registration number for your item. When you get the registration number, you know your item has been "posted" for sale.

Auction Fees: What you have to pay to sell your collectible

If you offer your antique or collectible on eBay or Amazon, you pay a nonrefundable "insertion fee," also called a "listing fee." If your item sells, you pay an additional "final value fee." The amount of the insertion fee depends on the type of listing you choose. Your listing can be a "regular listing," a "reserve price listing," or a "Dutch auction listing." You can also choose optional features for your listing, but each of the options adds to your fee. Most auctions charge all of these fees to the credit card you supplied when you registered as a seller.

INSERTION FEE

If you choose a "regular listing," you pay eBay a nonrefundable insertion fee based on your minimum bid. If your minimum bid is under $10, you pay 30 cents; if it's $50 or more, you pay the maximum fee, $3.30. There's a sliding scale in between.

DUTCH AUCTION INSERTION FEE

If you want to sell several identical items, your listing is referred to as a "Dutch listing." Your insertion fee is based on the minimum bid you set for a single item, multiplied by the number of identical items you're selling. If you're using eBay to sell five identical rhinestone butterfly pins and you set $25 as your opening value for a single pin, your insertion fee is $5.50 (five pins times $1.10, the insertion fee for a single item with an opening value of $25–$49.99). Bidders bid on the five pins separately at your auction, although a single bidder can bid on one, two, or all five. You may have to ship to five different successful bidders.

Once the bidding on an eBay Dutch auction is over, the winning bids are determined not only by the bid prices but also by the timing of the bids. For instance, if seven different bidders bid on your five butterfly pins, and the bids were $32, $30, $28, $26, $25, $25 and $25, you are obligated to sell each pin for $25 (the lowest winning bid becomes the selling price for all the items in a Dutch auction) to the four people who placed the highest bids and to the bidder who placed her $25 bid first.

Not all auction sites handle Dutch auctions this way. Some allow a seller to sell at the five highest prices bid on five identical items. Just be sure you understand the rules of the auction site you're using. Rules vary from site to site.

RESERVE FEE

If you set a "reserve price," a price below which you will not sell, then you pay an additional fee of 50 cents (if the reserve is under $25) or $1 (if it's $25 or more). *If your item sells, you don't pay the fee.*

EBay initiated reserve fees because some sellers were deliberately setting ridiculously high reserve prices just to see how high bidding would go. They would then go elsewhere (to another Internet site or to a shop) and offer the item for the highest price bids reached on eBay. EBay decided to charge reserve fees to discourage this practice.

BLESSED SUNDAYS

Many sellers of antiques and collectibles find that ending their auctions on Sunday evenings (not later than 11 P.M. ET) gives them the best opportunity for successful sales. Sunday is the day many people find extra time to spend at their home computers, bidding and buying.

EXTRA FEES

Some auction sites also provide escrow services, insurance programs, and secure credit card servers. Other auctions provide links to these types of services. Whether you take advantage of any of these services depends on what you are selling and how much you sell online. There are fees for some of these additional services.

FINAL VALUE FEE

Once your item has sold, eBay figures your "final value fee." It is based on the "final value" of your auctioned item. Your final value is the final sale price of your item. If you sold identical items in a Dutch listing, your final value is the lowest successful bid multiplied by the number of items you sold.

If your item sold for $25 or less, your fee is 5 percent of the sale price ($1.25 if your sale price was exactly $25). If your sale price was more than $25, the amount between $25 and $1,000 is

ESCROW SERVICES

Escrow services help protect buyers from fraud and mistakes, and help protect sellers from unscrupulous buyers. Escrow services are especially reassuring if you are selling or buying an expensive item. EBay and Amazon offer escrow services, but there are independent services too, such as I-Escrow. Escrow services function this way: The buyer sends payment to the escrow service instead of to the seller, and the escrow service holds the payment until the buyer inspects the merchandise and approves the purchase.

Most escrow services charge a 5 percent fee. Most of the time, the buyer pays the fee, but sometimes the seller pays or the fee is split between buyer and seller. If you are selling an item at an online auction, you can check off "escrow service" as a payment option when you list an item. Be sure your auction description explains who pays for the escrow service.

charged at 2.5 percent, and any part of the sale price above $1,000 is charged at 1.25 percent. If you received no bids for your item or if the bids did not meet your reserve, you are not charged a final value fee. You pay only your insertion fee, and a reserve fee if you set a reserve.

EBay is the largest of several Internet auctions that sell antiques and collectibles. The rules of other online auctions are similar to eBay's, but you'll want to read all of the instructions carefully, whatever auction you choose. We have included a chart at the end of the book comparing the three largest online auctions (eBay, Amazon, and Yahoo), and have supplied you with a list of other Internet sites you will find helpful—not only auctions, but also dealer malls, price lists, appraisal sites, auction-search services, and research sites.

What to Do After the Sale: Contact the buyer and finish the deal

Your item has sold to the highest bidder. EBay sends you an e-mail telling you that your item was sold and identifies the winning bidder by user name. You and the buyer must get in touch with each other by e-mail within three days. Most of the time, the

ONLINE AUCTION RULES FOR SELLERS:

1. Write clear, complete, and honest descriptions.
2. Answer e-mails quickly while your auction is going on.
3. Be reasonable in setting your payment terms.
4. Charge reasonable, fair amounts for shipping.
5. Ship promptly.
6. E-mail the buyer as soon as you ship.
7. If a problem arises, work with the buyer to reach a mutually agreeable solution.

seller e-mails the buyer first, but the buyer may contact you first. As the seller, you review what you charge for shipping and what payment methods you accept (you already listed this information in the description, but you have to go over it again after the sale). The buyer e-mails you to tell you where to ship. The buyer is also supposed to mail you a check or money order (or submit credit card information online or by phone) within a week after your e-mails are exchanged.

You, the seller, wait until you receive payment before you ship. If you have agreed to take a personal check, make sure the check clears before you ship. If the buyer sends you a money order, you can ship as soon as you receive payment. If your item is expensive, you and the buyer could agree to use an online escrow service (eBay, Amazon, and others offer access to escrow services).

Once you are paid, ship the item to the buyer via U.S. mail, UPS, FedEx, or another carrier. If you are like most sellers, you charged the buyer a fee for shipping, so pay for shipping at your end.

If you are shipping a delicate item, you may want to use a packing service like Mail Boxes Etc. to wrap, box, and send the item to the buyer. If you box items yourself, use sturdy corrugated cardboard boxes and bubble wrap, air bags, or Styrofoam "peanuts." If the item is breakable, use double boxes with Styrofoam peanuts surrounding the inside box.

E-mail the buyer when you ship, and ask the buyer to e-mail you as soon as the item arrives safely. Post positive feedback about the buyer, and ask the buyer to post positive feedback about you.

What Not to Do If You're Selling Online

1 It is not ethical to use an Internet auction to list an item you are offering in another auction or selling in a shop. Anything you post on an Internet auction must be exclusively available to that auction's buyers during the period of the auction. If you own

a shop full of collectible dolls and want to auction one Shirley Temple doll on the Internet, you must take Shirley off the shop's shelf while the auction is going on. If you own a Shirley Temple doll and have consigned it to an auction house, you cannot also offer it on the Internet. You also cannot offer it at two different auctions, traditional or online, at the same time.

[2] It is not ethical to renege on a sale once you have sold or bought an item. You cannot change your mind or back out without facing consequences. If you sell something and take payment, then fail to ship the item, you face criminal charges. If you sell something, then change your mind before you are paid, the would-be buyer is free to post comments about what you've done in the "Feedback" section of the auction. If you are a winning bidder in an auction but refuse to pay, the seller can post negative comments about you and at the same time follow the auction's formal complaint procedures. If you are a buyer who repeatedly reneges, the auction can label you a "non-paying bidder" and may eventually refuse to allow you to participate in auctions.

NON-PAYING BIDDERS

If a seller on eBay has not received payment within a reasonable period of time (7–14 days), the seller can do more than just post negative feedback. EBay provides a "Non-Paying Bidder Alert" form the seller can complete. EBay then e-mails the buyer a reminder to pay the seller. If the buyer still does not pay within the next 10 days, the seller can then submit a "Final Value Fee Credit" form to eBay so eBay can credit the seller for the costs of the aborted auction.

At the same time, any buyer whose nonpayment triggers three Final Value Fee (FVF) credits, whether affecting one or more sellers, is suspended from buying or selling on eBay for 30 days. A fourth FVF triggered by a buyer results in that buyer's permanent suspension from the auction.

3 It is not ethical (in fact, it is not legal) to post something for sale at an auction, then hire a shill (your spouse, friend, or coworker) to run up the bidding on your item. A shill is a bidder at an auction, whether online or traditional, who places bids just to drive up prices. The shill has no intention of buying the item. You cannot bid on your own item, either. Clues (*not* proof) that a shill is bidding:

- A shill bids aggressively until the high bid reaches the reserve, then suddenly stops bidding.

- If your bid was high but you were outbid, the seller contacts you and tells you the high bidder reneged and you can have the item after all. (You may still want the item, but don't be a fool. Offer the seller one increment over the *third-highest* bid.)

- An item was just listed and there is a surprising number of bids.

- If the suspected shill wins the bid, the same item shows up offered in a new auction by the same seller.

- The same bidder's user name shows up bidding at the seller's other auctions, but not at auctions of other sellers offering the same type of collectible.

Stay away from an auction that you suspect harbors a shill. If you are not sure, e-mail the bidder and nicely ask how long he has been interested in collecting Lladro figurines, for example. If you receive no reply, or if he sounds as though he knows absolutely nothing about Lladro, don't bid. And report your suspicions to the auction site.

Feedback

Online auctions want you to leave comments, positive or negative, about the sale or purchase you made on their site. If you are pleased with the way a seller treated you or the prompt way a buyer paid, post a positive note in "Feedback."

You can also post a negative comment if you are unhappy with any aspect of a sale—whether it's the seller's lack of promptness or the quality of the item. Negative feedback, however, is permanent, and should be considered a last resort. Think carefully before you post strong negative comments. Don't do it while you're angry. Retaliation can make you look bad.

Shills are at work in the feedback section, too. Some sellers use various screen names to post positive comments about themselves.

EBay feedback page.

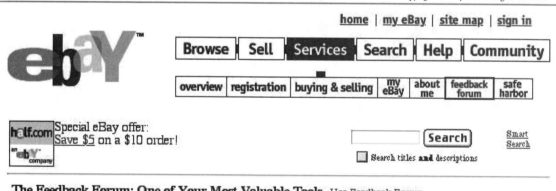

What to Sell

ONLINE BEST-SELLERS

Check your attic and basement for top cyber-selling antiques and collectibles. The Internet Antique Shop (www.tias.com) offers a monthly list of twenty items that sold best in the past thirty days. One month the list, in order, included Avon at No. 1, then Roseville, Noritake, cookie jars, china, dolls, McCoy, Limoges, Hull, Hummel, books, lamps, Carnival glass, coins, Depression

Tias Collector's Showcase page.

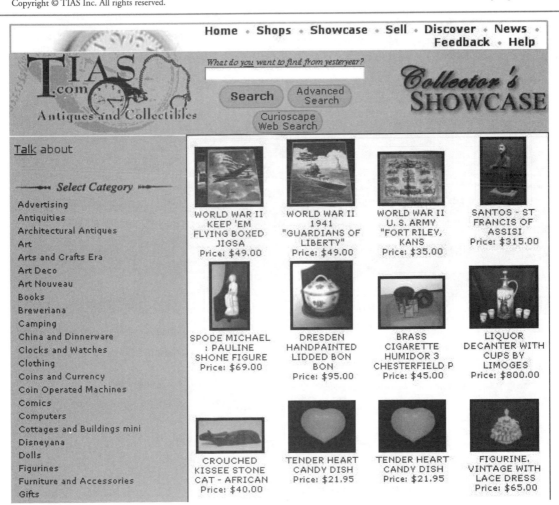

glass, plates, clocks, furniture, teapots, and Nippon. The next month, the list had changed slightly: Avon, Roseville, cookie jars, Noritake, Hull, dolls, McCoy, furniture, china, lamps, Limoges, Hummel, Carnival glass, books, clocks, plates, Depression glass, Royal Doulton, pottery, and teapots. Notice that from one month to the next, coins and Nippon disappeared from the list and Royal Doulton and pottery were added.

Some items remain favorites for a long time, or keep popping up on the Top Twenty list. On our Web site one recent month, we found a lot of people looking for information on Fostoria glass, Alexandrite, Hutschenreuther, Bossons, Phoenix birds, Crown Ducal, opera glasses, Buffalo pottery, coffee grinders, and scrimshaw, to name a few. We find that silver, china, furniture, vases, dolls, toys, and pottery are perennial online favorites.

FIVE THINGS THAT SELL BEST AT AN INTERNET AUCTION

1. **Out-of-print books.** Easy to describe, easy to ship, wanted by international buyers.

2. **Maps.** Easy to ship, popular as gifts, sell well to the area pictured on the map, which is often a long way from the seller's home.

3. **Recent out-of-production limited edition collectibles.** Items like Hummel figurines or Beanie Babies are easy to describe and well-known to prospective buyers. They're much harder to sell at flea markets and shops.

4. **Rare, well-authenticated sports collectibles.** The big spenders are shopping Internet auctions run by well-known sports collectibles dealers.

5. **One-of-a-kind, eccentric items.** The leprechaun-decorated center court floor used by the NBA's Boston Celtics was auctioned online for $331,100. Where else but online would you find the largest possible pool of potential buyers?

STUFF TO KEEP OFF THE INTERNET

You wouldn't take your old *Playboy* magazines to the church rummage sale—and there are things you shouldn't try to buy or sell on the Internet either. (You can, by the way, sell those *Playboys* on the Internet.) Yahoo found this out the hard way. One of its users offered Nazi artifacts for sale. The user didn't realize that it is illegal to sell Nazi artifacts in France. But the Internet is worldwide, so those items became available in France. Yahoo was sued by two advocacy groups in France and found guilty of "offending the country's collective memory."

Obviously, it is against the law to sell anything online that it is illegal to sell anywhere else. This list includes illegal drugs, endangered species, stolen goods, sex, people (dead or alive), and human organs.

More items you should be wary of posting for sale or buying: guns, explosives, erotica, pornography (not including old *Playboys*, obviously), cigarettes, and liquor. American Indian items are also touchy. Sales may break laws in some states. Some sites also bar the sale of police-related items, animals (dead or alive), human body parts, stock and stock certificates, and switchblades.

Yet the market varies online just as it does on land. Seasonal interest exists. Holiday items always sell best in the months just preceding the holiday. Sell Christmas ornaments starting in October. Sell Halloween decorations starting in September. Bring out the heart-shaped items for Valentine's Day in January. Small, gift-type items will sell well just before Christmas. Start selling flower and garden-oriented items in the early spring.

Fraud Problems for Sellers

WARNING: A seller we know auctioned a diamond necklace online. The buyer paid using an escrow service, then returned the necklace to the seller claiming that its quality was not as expected. The seller discovered that the diamonds in the necklace had been replaced with inferior stones. *Moral:* Don't sell diamonds on the Internet.

WARNING: Another seller we know auctioned a mint Weller vase online. The buyer returned the vase, claiming it was not mint at all but had glaze cracks and three chips on the base. The seller realized immediately that although the vase was the same pattern and size as the one he sold, it was *not* the same vase. *Moral:* Take clear, good-sized photographs of the item you're selling, from all angles. Some sellers attach self-destructing stickers to items to prevent this sort of "switching" fraud. The stickers shred if they're removed, and these sellers insist that the sticker be intact if an item is returned. If you are defrauded by a switch, your buyer was a crook. You must post negative feedback immediately. Tell the buyer you know what happened and that you are planning to file mail fraud charges against him. If you hear nothing, head for the post office.

WARNING: You will undoubtedly deal with buyers who do not pay after winning one of your items at auction. Try, via e-mail, to discover what the problem is or to persuade the buyer to pay you. If, after two weeks, you receive no payment or explanation, post negative feedback about the buyer and refuse to take bids from this buyer in the future. Many online auctions will credit your account for the final value fee you were charged when the auction ended. Wait a few months before trying to sell the item again.

WARNING: Sellers have been taken by fraudulent buyers, even when an escrow service was used. A case described in the *New York Times* involved a seller who shipped an expensive watch to a buyer once the escrow service had received the buyer's credit card payment. Right after the watch was dropped off at the post office for shipment, the escrow service e-mailed the seller to tell her they had just discovered that the buyer had used a stolen credit card. Legal authorities intervened, stopped shipment of the watch, and eventually arrested and jailed the teenaged "buyer."

REMEMBER: Print and save copies of every e-mail exchanged between you and the buyer.

TAKING PRECAUTIONS AGAINST CREDIT CARD FRAUD

There are several intelligent precautions to take against credit card fraud if you sell using online auctions:

1. Ship the item only to the billing address for the credit card. Anyone using a stolen card will not want you to do this. The credit card billing address can be confirmed by the escrow service or by the company handling the online credit card payment.

2. Don't sell to a buyer who is in too big a hurry. If a buyer wants to close a sale before an auction ends or asks to pay for overnight shipping, be wary.

3. Be wary of buyers who use free e-mail services such as Hotmail, Bigfoot, Excite or Yahoo. It's easier for buyers to hide their real identities with a free service.

4. Don't let a credit card buyer make small payments over time. Credit card companies tend to pay more attention to large charges than small ones.

5. Use escrow and credit card services that offer guarantees against fraudulent credit card users. This can involve time-consuming verification processes when you set up your account, but taking the extra time is worthwhile.

ADDICTION WARNING

A friend of ours who collects Torquay pottery mottoware had to quit buying on eBay "cold turkey." She found herself spending more money—and time—online than she could afford. Another friend was ordered to quit by the lawyer who handled her trust when he saw how much money she was spending online.

It is easy to lose hours browsing an online auction or even surfing the Internet. If you're also spending money you don't want to spend, don't mean to spend, and can't afford to spend, you have become an addict. If your problem is not very serious but you're worried about what could happen, put yourself on a "therapy" program that limits the time and money you spend online.

Budget your money and your time wisely, so you aren't forced to quit doing something you really enjoy. Like a careful gambler, spend only what you want to spend—not more.

Tax Consequences

If you wind up using Internet auctions to buy cheap and sell high, you may owe the IRS taxes on your earnings. Any profit you make selling something may have to be reported as a capital gain on Schedule D of your tax return. Talk to your tax advisor.

If you start buying and selling regularly at a profit, the IRS may consider what you're doing a business, not a hobby. You may have to report your profits as income on Schedule C of your tax return. If your income from your "business" is more than $400 a year, you have to pay self-employment taxes. Again, talk to your tax advisor.

The benefits of considering your hobby a business are that you can deduct expenses like shipping costs, packing materials, online fees, and the cost of your Internet service. (The IRS will question these deductions if they exceed your income after you have been in business three to five years.) You may even be able to write off a home office, but the rules for that are complicated.

At this point, the IRS is investigating only large-scale vendors who use Internet auctions, but the agency is aware that many Internet sales go unreported. At some point, the IRS will probably develop a computerized tracking system to follow electronic trails to unreported income.

Currently, state and local sales tax does not have to be collected on items sold via online person-to-person auctions. This may change someday.

A Seller's Diary

MONDAY

8:00 A.M.   Get up bright and early to continue my ongoing basement-cleaning project.

10:00   Realize, with exhaustion, that there is just too much stuff to keep. Hey, didn't I see Lucite resin grapes for sale on eBay the other day? I could sell mine.

11:00   I've bought things before on eBay, so I'm already registered. Decide to sell the set (a bunch of green Lucite resin grapes and two matching candlesticks). Wash grapes lightly to remove most of the dust.

11:05   Take a Polaroid picture using a white sheet for background. If I'm going to unload these things quickly, I don't want to wait for film from a regular 35-mm camera to be processed.

11:10   While the picture is developing, I look at eBay to see going prices. Seems like $9.99 is a good starting price. My grapes have matching candleholders; they should be more attractive to buyers.

11:20   Photo is finished. The color is off a bit, but I will explain it in the description.

11:25   Measure the items (8 in. L., 4$\frac{1}{2}$ in. w., candleholders,
4 in. each side of triangle), look for damage
(fabric leaves need to be replaced), no markings except
for labels on candleholders: "Caution: Manufacturer
not responsible for damage due to candle burning
below level of the resin balls." Round up a box.
Items weigh 3$\frac{1}{2}$ pounds in box.

11:40   Ready to list. Find out I have to submit my
credit card number for ID purposes even though
I'm already a registered buyer. I have never sold
anything before and this policy was added
since I registered.

11:45   Had to re-log on to computer, slow connection.

11:50   Secure credit card listing page failed to come up.
Decide to try to find different link to page.
Find one in the "Selling" section on the site map.

11:55   Form crashed again and I receive a message saying
"This functionality is currently unavailable."

11:55   Decide not to waste any more time and to write
description so I'll be ready when server is up.
I open up a word processing page and type my
description. I'll copy and paste it into eBay's
"Sell" form when the time comes.

12:10 P.M.   Check out the post office rate calculator online (www.usps.com) to establish shipping and handling cost, including insurance; $5.50 seems fair.

12:15   I attempt my third try to list credit card. Their system finally accepts the form this time.

12:16   Now a page comes up telling me I have to wait for e-mail with notice of account approval.

12:20   I'll keep plugging along with the preparation.
I scan Polaroid photo and save it as JPEG file.

12:22   Post the scanned photo using an FTP program to my personal Web page, which came with the e-mail account I set up with my ISP.

12:25   I go to the Web page to make sure the scan looks good and to copy the full URL for the JPEG. I paste the URL (http://pages.prodigy.net/username/forsale/resingrapes.jpg) into my description document.

12:27   Description complete, with a couple HTML codes added to make bold type and breaks between paragraphs.
I had to abbreviate candleholders in the title (the limit is 45 characters), but I don't think this will affect people's ability to search for the auction page. They'll be looking for "resin grapes" or "Lucite."

TITLE: Retro Green Lucite Resin Grapes and Candlehldrs

DESCRIPTION: Dress up your Formica coffee table with this vintage green resin grape centerpiece set. The grapes have a painted driftwood stem and plastic leaves (which need to be replaced due to age, an easy trip to the craft store). Unlike other resin grape bunches I've seen, this set has matching triangular 3-ball candleholders.

The color is a little off in the photo, the resin balls are all a rich avocado green. The grape bunch is 8 1/2 inches long and 4 1/2 inches wide. The candleholder bases are 4 inches on each side. Both are labeled "Caution: Manufacturer not responsible for damage due to candle burning below level of the resin balls." I put candles in the candleholders for effect. They're old and dirty, but you can have them if you want them.

Buyer will pay shipping & handling fee of $5.50, including insurance. Payment by money order please. Items will ship by Priority Mail within two days of receipt of payment. Please e-mail me with questions.

PHOTO URL: http://pages.prodigy.net/username/forsale/resingrapes.jpg

12:28	Still waiting for account update. I go back to the credit card listing page to see if there is anything I overlooked. Now I notice that eBay says it may take 24 hours to verify credit card!
12:30	Decide to eat lunch.
1:00	Still no word from eBay.
2:15	Still no word, so I decide to try to fill out the "Sell" form anyhow. Maybe the notice of approval is just a formality.
2:20	Nope, they won't let me sell my grapes until my credit card is processed.
2:45	Blow off some steam by sending an e-mail to eBay asking why it takes so long to verify my credit card. Noticed that their announcement board said something about intermittent server trouble. Maybe that's why I'm having so much trouble.
3:03	Finally receive approval. Return to "Sell" form. Copy and paste my title, description, and photo URL into the appropriate fields. I click on all the boxes that apply to my sale to put check marks in them. Hit the "Review my auction listing" button; a summary of the checked boxes shows up with a preview of my description and photo as they will appear.

3:05	I notice a typo, so I hit my browser's "Back" button to go fix it on the original "Sell" form. Then I hit the "Review" button again, but this time I get an error message. I forgot to reenter my password after I fixed the typo. Hit the "Back" button again, reenter the password, hit the "Review" button again. Everything works OK this time, looks good, so I hit the "Submit my listing" button.
3:08	The auction has begun! A page comes up that confirms my listing information and description and assigns me an auction number. I print the page for my records.
5:00	Log on anxiously to check if there are any bids. EBay's search engine doesn't list new auction pages immediately, so I probably can't search for it.
5:03	I'll find it a different way. I go to eBay's search page and click on the "find item by number" tab. I enter my auction page number in the window.
5:04	The page comes up. Shucks, no bids yet.

TUESDAY

2:03 P.M.	Log on to see if my listing is showing up in eBay's search. I type "resin grapes" in the search window on the home page.

2:04   A total of 20 resin grapes bunches come up for sale.
            My auction is there. It still hasn't received any bids,
            but neither have 12 other resin grapes auctions.

WEDNESDAY

10:00 A.M. I log on to eBay, click on "My eBay" at the top of
            the screen and click on the "selling" tab. There's a link
            to my auction. I click on it. No bids. Decide I'll wait a
            couple days before I look again.

FRIDAY

7:00 P.M.   OK, so I'm too anxious to wait any longer. Log on to
            check out my auction.

7:03   Eureka, a bid! Only one bid, but at least I'm getting
            $9.99 for my dusty grapes. Now I can relax a little.

SATURDAY

2:00 P.M.   Log on again. No more bids. Sheesh!

MONDAY, WEEK 2

10:45 AM   Log on. This is the last day of my sale. I didn't get
            to check the auction yesterday because I was outdoors
            with my family.

10:48   No more bids. Current price is still $9.99. Maybe some-
one will come in at the last minute and snipe him.
The auction ends at 5:08 P.M., my time. I'll have to check
after I get home. Better get back to work.

11:48pm   Darn kids! I am just now logging on the computer to
check my auction that ended hours ago.

11:55   Auction ended with only one bid for $9.99. Oh well,
it's more than I would have been paid at a garage sale.

TUESDAY, WEEK 2

12:07AM   Send an e-mail to successful bidder with cordial
greeting and total cost ($9.99 for grapes and candle-
holders plus $5.50 for shipping and insurance; total is
$15.49). It's late; I know I won't hear from him for a
while. I'm going to bed.

WEDNESDAY, WEEK 2

11:45AM   No reply from sender.

7:00p.m.   No reply from sender. It's summer; maybe he's on
vacation. If he's an antiques dealer, he might be out of
town at a show.

THURSDAY, WEEK 2

11:45 A.M. Still no reply from bidder and I'm getting worried. I always contact the seller the day the auction ends, sometimes before they contact me. I think I'll send another message. I'll say I was having e-mail problems and will ask if he received my message. This time I'll ask him to confirm that he received my e-mail message.

1:22 P.M. A reply at last, typed hastily in all lowercase letters with no punctuation. He asks if I take PayPal or checks; if not he'll have to put a money order in the mail tomorrow. I'm a bit irritated because I clearly stated in both the listing information and in my description that I prefer a money order for payment. I look at his feedback rating to see if he's ever backed out on a seller.

1:28 He has a great feedback record with more than 900 positive comments. I think I can trust a check from him. What the heck.

1:30 Send a reply to his e-mail message saying I'll accept a check and thanking him for his quick response to my second message.

MONDAY, WEEK 3

11:25 A.M. The check arrives. It's postmarked the 3rd, so he didn't get to the post office any sooner with the check than he would have if he'd used a money order.

11:30   Send an e-mail acknowledging the payment and thanking him for a smooth transaction. I tell him I'll leave positive feedback and hope he is happy with the grapes (implying, of course, that I want him to leave positive feedback for me).

12:37 P.M. I go to the My eBay page again and click on the "Selling" tab, then I click on the grapes auction link. On the auction page there is a "Leave Feedback" link. I click on seller and it takes me directly to a form with the item number and the bidder's name already filled in. I'm not overly thrilled with his transaction, but I leave a positive comment: "Good response, quick payment, reliable bidder."

5:15 P.M. The check goes into my bank account.

TUESDAY, WEEK 3

9:00 A.M. I pack up the grapes. My husband says a tearful good-bye, then I wrap the pieces individually in bubble wrap and surround them in foam peanuts. Luckily I have a Priority Mail shipping box from another eBay purchase that I can reuse for this sale.

9:15   Debating whether to ship today or not. I asked for a money order and would have shipped immediately if I had received one. Should I wait for the check to clear? I think I'll wait a day or two.

THURSDAY, WEEK 3

8:30 A.M. Take the package to the post office. I didn't calculate the postage very well last week. It turns out it will cost me $6.50 to send the box by Priority Mail (which I promised in my auction description). Oh well, there goes another $1 of my profit.

8:45 The grapes are on their way.

MONDAY, WEEK 4

10:15 A.M. E-mail message from my bidder: Package arrived intact, grapes are exactly what he expected. That's a load off my mind. He promises to leave me positive feedback.

7:30 P.M. Log on to eBay to check for the feedback. It's there. "Praise: Shipment arrived on time and in good condition. Service & packaging good." Well, that wasn't so bad. Now, what can I unload next?

PART FOUR

Online
Hotline

Online Record Breakers

Record prices for antiques and collectibles are set every year. Now that Internet auctions are available and can reach an ever-expanding market, prices for some rare items are hitting new peaks. The following records were set at recent online auctions.

In 1989 a Philadelphia man bought a picture frame for $4 at a flea market. It held an old, torn painting. He wanted to frame another picture, so he removed the painting and discovered a piece of paper folded up behind it. The paper was a copy of the Declaration of Independence. He quite reasonably assumed it was one of the reproductions floating around, but was persuaded to show it to an expert at Sotheby's, the New York auction house. It was declared an authentic original copy of a July 4–5, 1776, printing of the Declaration of Independence. Copies like it were hung on buildings and posts around the colonies to let the public know that independence had been declared. (The story is that the fellow who sold him the painting knew the document was there and *also* assumed it was fake.)

The document—called the Dunlap Broadside after Philadelphia printer John Dunlap—is one of only twenty-five known surviving copies of the first printing of the Declaration of Independence. The copy, in wonderful condition, sold at a live auction in 1991 for $2.4 million. It broke the auction record for printed Americana. When it sold again on June 29, 2000—this time online—it brought $8.14 million and shattered records for both printed Americana and Internet auctions.

The original, signed Declaration of Independence, by the way, is stored in an inert helium atmosphere in Washington, D.C.—a far cry from the atmosphere behind an old painting.

———

A Honus Wagner baseball card set records at an Internet auction and attracted other sellers of "Wagner" cards. Only about fifty of the 1909 American Tobacco Company cards picturing the Pittsburg Pirates Hall of Fame shortstop are known to exist (Pittsburgh was spelled without a final *h* from December 23, 1891 to July 19, 1911). The Wagner card is part of the T206 tobacco card set, the most collected set of baseball cards ever.

The auctioned card was once owned by hockey star Wayne Gretzky and Bruce McNall, owner of the NHL Los Angeles Kings. Gretzky and McNall paid a record $461,000 for it in 1991. The card was later sold to Wal-Mart, which raffled it off in a promotion. The Wal-Mart winner, a Miami mail carrier, auctioned the card in 1996 through Christie's of New York. It sold for a record $640,500. It sold again in July 2000 for a record $1.265 million via an online auction jointly sponsored by eBay and Robert Edward Auctions.

This particular card was rare, popular, and had a well-documented history. It is considered the finest specimen of the fifty known cards.

While we were checking on results on the day the sale ended, we found two other eBay sellers purporting to sell the rare card. One seller was requesting $300,000 in cash for a card that was torn and had been folded. Her description was this: *Little scuffy and a tear in the upper right corner. In overall good condition! See picture for more. Cash Please.* No one bid on that card.

The other seller titled the offered card: "Honus Wagner T-206, probably the real one." It had no picture, but an amusing description that said in part: *This is the card with a great value. I don't know if it's the real one but my grandfather gave to me this card before he die. So it's a risk for the buyer. . . . On the back there is nothing. I think the card was in a scrapbook and the dealers said to me a word like trim [the card may have been trimmed] I think . . . I think it's a painting on the card.* The seller set a reserve price, which was met after 47 bids. The sale closed with the highest bid at $1,025. Sometimes buyers like to gamble. Then again, neither the buyer nor the seller in this case left feedback on eBay. So the sale may or may not have been completed.

The most expensive toy yet sold on the Internet was a rare tinplate battleship. Made in 1902 by Marklin, a top German toy manufacturer, the battleship had been played with by several generations of the Reginald Phillips family in the United Kingdom. HMS *Resolution* is a hand-painted twin-masted battleship, 39¾ inches long, meant for use in the water. A UK dealer bought the toy through Sotheby's online auction for $44,660. The record was set April 12, 2000.

A Fire-King–crazy collector paid $1,010 for a single 5-ounce Jade-ite ruffled-rim custard cup in a May 1999 online auction. The Anchor Hocking cup is one of only two known to exist. Only a few collectors knew what a treasure it was. The seller had a reserve of $30.

One Man's Trash Is Another Man's Treasure

Don't throw it away! Not every sale will be a record breaker, but some people have found that their trash sells for treasurelike prices online. A Pennsylvania man sold a nonworking 1970 Movado Tachymetre watch with a scratched crystal for $450 on eBay. A Nebraska woman got $300 for an old, faded, and cracked wooden checkerboard she had bought for $1.

Online Auction Tales

Buying and selling online can be profitable, practical, and just plain fun. It can also be unnerving. Here are some true stories about online auctions. Some serve as warnings. Others are encouraging. Still others will make you laugh.

BREAD CRUMBS

Last year, we bought a strip of fifty bread wrappers from an Internet auction for $10. A bakery had closed and a smart collector found hundreds of items in the store's trash, including old signs, huge rolls of waxed paper bread wrappers printed with a colorful logo, and the stickers that were used to close the ends of the bread wrapper. Knowing it was all collectible, she trucked it home and started selling small batches online. We got a bargain for our packaging collection, and she made money on all of the paper collectibles.

THE MODERN PAINTING HOAX

In May 2000, an eBay seller offered a modern painting he said he had picked up at a yard sale. The signature on the painting, "RD '52," led some bidders to believe it was the work of California abstract painter Richard Diebenkorn, who died in 1993. A Dutch collector bid $138,805, but eBay voided the sale because the seller had bid on the painting himself (in other words, he acted as a shill for himself). It turned out the seller had also misrepresented the history of the painting.

A GEM OF A STORY

A jeweler placed a rare brown diamond in his online auction with an asking price of $1.2 million. When bidding ended, he thought it had sold and that he had brokered the most expensive gem sale in online history.

The buyer offered $200,000 cash for the gem and what he described as a historic Pennsylvania mansion once lived in by steel magnate Charles Schwab. The jeweler made the sale contingent on an appraisal of the mansion. Thank goodness. He found out the "historic mansion" was actually an old, run-down school building Schwab built and named for his wife. No sale there!

SOPHIE'S BUTTERFLY

Lee thought his daughter Sophie's room should have a butterfly stool designed by Sori Yanagi in the 1950s. Originals sell for $3,000 to $4,000 at Modernism shows. New stools, still made by the original Japanese manufacturer, Tendo Mokko Co., sell for $725. Lee decided to try eBay. He found a seller offering an old reissue of the stool in rosewood. His bid won him a "bargain" in great condition for $400. No shipping charges, either. The seller lived less than a half hour away, so Lee drove over to get his prize.

If you plan to pick up or drop off an item in person, do take some reasonable precautions. Know who you're meeting, know where you're going, go during daylight hours, don't meet in a secluded spot, and take a friend with you.

WITCHES

Donna collects Royal Doulton Witches pattern dishes. Her collection started with a single bowl given to her by her grandmother. The pattern was made from 1906 to 1928, and only a few different pieces were produced. Each pictured a witch with a cauldron. At every antiques show she could find, she asked about her dishes. But in twenty years, she had only four pieces.

Then came Internet auctions. In two years she has found ten more pieces, most purchased from sellers in England and other countries in Europe. Internet auctions are international and sometimes a rare piece in the United States is plentiful abroad.

FUN HOUSE

An Ohio collector who lives near an amusement park that was sold last summer has been shopping on eBay for memorabilia related to the old park, called Geauga Lake. He usually searches eBay using the words "amusement park." He changed his search one time and tried, simply, "Geauga." He found an old plate picturing the park and won it for just $5. The seller had posted it in eBay's Collector Plate subcategory rather than under Circus, Carnival, where many amusement park items are found. The Ohio collector is sure it would have gone for at least $30 if it had been posted in the Circus, Carnival subcategory.

DEANNA DURBIN REMEMBERED

A reporter friend called and said: "After I wrote a magazine article about the Kovels at a flea market, I remembered the Deanna Durbin doll that I lost long ago as a child. Is there anyplace I can find one?"

We checked all the regular doll auctions and had no luck. "Why not try an online auction?" we asked her. She thought that sounded like a great learning experience. A few weeks later, she called back and reported:

"I got my doll and it's beautiful. I stayed up till three in the morning to get the last bid and it worked. The seller is an elderly dealer who has been out of business for fifteen years. She thought her dolls were still worth the same amount they were fifteen years ago, so she set low opening-bid prices. It must have scared off some of the bidders, because I got Deanna for half the doll price guide price and she is in almost mint condition."

STAR QUALITY

A collector one day tried searching among eBay items for his own name. He found an autographed photo of a 1940s movie star who happened to share his name. He bought the photo for just a couple of dollars and is having lots of fun showing it off.

Online Auction Sample Prices

There's nothing like online auctions to help you sell stuff no one touched at your last garage sale. Or stuff that's worth more somewhere else in the country than it is in your neighborhood. Or stuff you've stored in your attic for decades, thinking you'd probably throw it away someday. Take a look at these real prices for the odds and ends people have bought online.

CRAZY FOR THE KITCHEN—Art Deco–style chrome automatic Sunbeam toaster, $23.50; chrome and Bakelite General Electric toaster with weather vane motif, $9.95; 1947 magazine ad for Toastmaster toaster with Santa Claus, $2.99; 9-inch Dazey electric glass jar mixer, $31.10; Avocado green Kitchen Aid stand mixer with attachments, $105.99; 1951 General Electric catalog with Triple Whip mixer, toaster, roaster, grill, waffle iron, and irons, $7.

PAINTING BY THE NUMBERS—1980 *Star Wars* paint-by-number sets, Luke, $20.50, Han Solo, $18.01, Yoda, $15.72; framed 1967 paint-by-number still life, $6.50.

KEEP 'EM IN STITCHES—1940s wicker sewing basket with applied roses, $32.50; vintage sewing basket filled with 1950s needle books and other sewing accessories, $15.50; clear green Bakelite buttons, 4 on card, $3.75; 1930s pearl shirt buttons on card, $5; Czechoslovakian emerald green glass buttons, 12 on card, $8; Bakelite Scottie dog buttons, 6 on card, $41.40; 8-foot length of tan and gray barkcloth, "Happily Married" pattern, $129.49; 1960s cotton printed with purple, pink, pea green, and yellow circles, 1½ yards, $20; 1930s piqué cotton with grapes & leaves, 4 yards, $23.40.

POODLE PANDEMONIUM—Turquoise and white poodle painted on velvet, 12 x 9 inches, $6; wicker sewing basket with black felt poodle, $9.99; gold-tone metal and mesh purse with applied poodles and painted Eiffel Tower scene, $29.

DRESSED TO THE NINES—1970s pewter metallic leather purse, $4.25; painted oak splint basket purse, $30; 1920s lace evening bag with rhinestone ball clasp, $31.50; two-tone alligator purse, $36.75; 1940s pink shirtwaist dress, $36; 1950s swing dress, 2 bows, Gigi Young, $13.50; 1970s polyester dress, red & blue print, $9.99.

HOT & SMOKING—Charles Denby cigar box, Diamond Joe Cigar Factory, $35; Totem cigar box, 1923, $9.99; Fuente cigar box, red silk inside lid, $10.10.

MAKE-IT-YOURSELF COLLECTIBLES—1920s Dennison sealing wax craft kit, $11.28; Royal Society tie-rack craft kit, 1926; Revell Chris-Craft Flying Bridge Cruiser boat kit, 1953, $7; Skil Craft microscope lab, 1963, $3.99; Walco Charm Craft pearl jewelry kit, 1950, $42.99; Toy Corporation pattern kit with fabric, shoes, and accessories for 13-inch fashion doll, 1968, $24.

RESURRECTED FROM RESTAURANTS—Sterling China U.S. Marine Corps sugar, 2 handles, $20.50; Shenango morning glory cup & saucer, $28; Tepco tan 14-inch platter, $15.51.

DECORATING DETAILS—Decorating book by *Ladies' Home Journal,* 1959, $20.50; Dux Furniture catalog, Sweden, 1966, $22.95; 1904 plumbing supply catalog, hardbound, 864 pages, $377; 1940 Sears Roebuck catalog, $51.01.

FOR THE RECORD—"Yesterday" LP record, The Beatles, Australian pressing, $14.03; "A Hard Day's Night" LP record, The Beatles, $13.83; "Hey Jude" LP record, The Beatles, $5.70; Beatles 45 RPM record holder, 1966, $212.50; "My Way" 45 RPM record, Elvis Presley, picture sleeve, $2.26; "Love Me Tender" 45 RPM record, Elvis Presley, $2.50; "Viva Las Vegas" 45 RPM extended play record, $8.50; velvet painting, Elvis in white jumpsuit, 24 x 35 inches, $91.

COMPARISON OF THREE AUCTION SITES

FEATURES	AMAZON	EBAY	YAHOO
Registration (not required for browsing on most sites)	• You are preregistered if you are already a customer of Amazon.com (i.e., if you have bought books from Amazon). • If not, you have to give your name, e-mail and street addresses, phone number, and a credit card number.	• Initial registration requires your name, e-mail and street addresses, and phone number. • Credit card number required when selling and for anyone with an anonymous e-mail address.	• Only requires selection of user name and password. • Contact information and credit card number required when selling.
Buying	• No fee. • Automatic proxy bidding (bid-click). • Going, Going, Gone feature: Auction continues 10 minutes after latest bid. • Amazon.com Payments (1-click) option: Buyer can pay some sellers with credit card online; no fee.	• No fee. • Automatic proxy bidding. • Billpoint Online Payments option: Buyer can pay some sellers online with credit card or from checking account; no fee.	• No fee. • Straight bidding or automatic proxy bidding. • Yahoo Pay Direct option: Buyer can pay online with credit card or from checking account; no fee.

FEATURES	AMAZON	EBAY	YAHOO
Buying (continued)	• Protected by Amazon's A-to-Z Guarantee for purchases from qualified sellers (designated by A-to-Z logo). Maximum coverage is $250; $1,000 for Amazon.com Payments (see above). • Escrow service available.	• Protected by insurance from Lloyd's of London for items that sold for at least $25 by a qualified seller. Maximum coverage is $200, less a $25 deductible. • Escrow service available.	• No support for disputes between buyer and seller.
Bid Retraction	• Allowed only for typos in bid or for misrepresentation by seller. Subject to review, can't bid again on same item.	• Allowed for typos and misrepresentation by seller. Bidder can re-bid on same item.	• Bidder cannot cancel bid; can ask seller to cancel bid.
Selling	• Listing fee: 10¢. Additional fees apply for optional features like boldface type. • Photo hosting: free, limited to one 100KB image.	• Insertion Fee: 30¢ to $3.30, based on the opening bid. Additional fees apply for optional features like boldface type. • Photo hosting: first two images free; additional images allowed at 50¢ each.	• Listing fee: 20¢ to $1.50, based on the opening bid. Additional fee applies for featured auction status (higher amount gives higher placement on list). • Photo hosting: free, limited to three images, 1.5MB total size.

FEATURES	AMAZON	EBAY	YAHOO
Selling (continued)	• Completion Fee: up to $25 is 5%; $25.01–$1,000 is $1.25 plus 2.5%; over $1,000 is $25.63 plus 1.25%.	• Final Value Fee: 5% for first $25 of selling price, plus 2.5% for $25.01 to $1,000, plus 1.25% for amount over $1,000.	• No final value fees.
	• Bulk Loader program available for entering multiple listings.	• Mister Lister program available for entering multiple listings.	• Auction Express program available for entering multiple listings.
	• Pro Merchant Tools for heavy users.	• Power Trader services for heavy users.	• Merchant Auctions program for heavy users.
	• No reserve price fee.	• Reserve price fee charged if item doesn't sell (50¢ for price set below $25; $1 for prices at or above $25).	• Reserve price fee charged if item doesn't sell (40¢ for price set below $25; 75¢ for prices at or above $25).
	• No fee for relisting items that don't sell.	• No fee for relisting items that don't sell.	• Auto-resubmission relists items that don't sell.
	• Amazon.com Payments (1-click) option: Seller can accept credit cards online; fee.	• Billpoint Online Payments option: Seller can accept credit cards or electronic checks online; fee.	• Yahoo PayDirect: Seller can accept credit cards or electronic checks; no fee.
	• Escrow service available.	• Escrow service available.	
	• Sellers protected by Back-Out Buyers policy.	• Sellers protected by Non-Paying Bidders policy.	

FEATURES	AMAZON	EBAY	YAHOO
Editing or Canceling Auction	• Seller can change description until first bid. Afterward, can add information. • Seller can only cancel auction if there are no bidders. Can close early, but must honor bids.	• Seller can revise anything before first bid. Afterward, can add information. • Seller can cancel bids, then close auction. Can close early, but must honor bids.	• Seller can add new information. • Seller can cancel bids, then close auction. Can close early, but must honor bids.
Feedback	• Buyers and sellers rate each other with 1 to 5 stars. Average star rating appears next to user name. Feedback profile also shows number of cancelled bids.	• Buyers and sellers rate each other with positive (+1), neutral (0), or negative (-1) comments. Total of comment points appears next to user name.	• Buyers and sellers rate each other with positive (+1), neutral (0), or negative (-1) comments. Total of comment points appears next to user name.
Special Options	• Member Profile Pages: Users have a link to a page that lists auctions and feedback. • First-Bidder Discount: The first bidder receives a 10% discount if he is the high bidder at the end of the auction.	• Personal Shopper: Users can save their favorite searches or can request e-mail notification of items that match favorite searches. • My eBay: Users can create a page with links to feedback, favorite categories, items that have been bid on or are for sale, and items to watch.	• Auction Alert: Notifies user of auctions in favorite category, by seller or by keyword. • Minimum Bidder Rating: Sellers can choose whether bidders are required to submit credit card numbers with their bids.

FEATURES	AMAZON	EBAY	YAHOO
Special Options (continued)	• zShop: Users can post items for fixed-price sales.	• About Me: Users can create a Web page with personal or business information.	• Blacklist: Seller can prevent specific users from bidding.
	• Authentication, grading, and appraisal services available with discounted fees.	• Safe Harbor: Authentication, grading, appraisal, and user verification services.	• Auto-Extension: Auction continues 5 minutes after latest bid.
	• Take-It Price: Sellers can set a price that will end the auction.	• Buy-It-Now price: Seller can set a price that will end the auction.	• Buy Price: Sellers can set a price that will end the auction.
			• Early Close: Sellers can end the auction when satisfied with the bid price.

GLOSSARY

NOTE: Many of the acronyms listed here are not yet included in standard dictionaries.

Bid shielding: An unethical practice similar to a dealer ring at a live auction. Two or more online bidders work together to keep prices low. One bidder bids low. The second bidder bids extremely high, then retracts his bid at the last minute. The first bidder wins the item at the low price.

Bid siphoning: Using posted bidder information to sell items privately without an auction. Online auctions try to protect their users' identities.

Bookmarking: Storing the Web addresses of your favorite Web sites so you can get to them quickly. When you open a Web page you want to bookmark, you click on the "Bookmark" or "Add to Favorites" icon.

Browser: Software that navigates the World Wide Web (Internet). You need a browser to view Web pages.

CD-ROM: A compact disc with "Read Only Memory." The disc looks like a music CD. You insert it in the CD-ROM drive on your computer, and your computer can either run software on the CD or load it on your hard drive. A CD-RW is a compact disc that is readable and writable.

Clicking: Pressing a button on your computer mouse.

Cut, Copy, Paste: Editing functions that allow you to cut or copy words or documents and paste them into another sentence or document.

Double-clicking: Two quick clicks on a mouse button.

Dutch auction: A person-to-person auction of several identical items. Bidders bid on one or more of the items.

E-mail: Electronic mail sent over the Internet.

Encryption: The coding of information sent over the Internet to make it difficult for an unauthorized person to find and read it.

Favorites: See Bookmarking.

Feedback: Comments left by one person about another after completing an online auction transaction.

FTP: Acronym for File Transfer Protocol, used to post data to another location (e.g., on the Web).

Home page: The main page of a Web site, which comes up first when you go to the site.

HTML: Acronym for Hypertext Markup Language, the coding language used to create Web pages.

Hyperlink: Words or photos on a Web page that, when clicked, take you to another page or site. Hyperlink words are underlined and in a different font color. When you pass the cursor over the words, the arrow changes into a little hand. Click your mouse button and the linked page opens on your screen. (Also called a "link.")

Image file: A JPEG (.jpg) or GIF (.gif) file that contains a graphic image or photograph. JPEG files usually contain a photo; GIF files, an image.

Internet: A collection of networks that allows computers around the world to communicate with each other. Also called the Net.

ISP: Internet Service Provider. A business that provides Internet access to the public.

JPEG: Acronym for Joint Photographic Experts Group; an image file used for photographs.

Keywords: Descriptive words and phrases used to instruct search engines to perform tasks, such as locating Web sites or auction listings.

Link: *See* Hyperlink.

Maximum bid: The most you will bid for an item up for auction. Once you enter your maximum bid, you can raise it but you can't lower it. Used when your bidding is handled automatically by the online auction.

Minimum bid: The amount at which bidding starts in an online auction.

Modem: Hardware that enables two networked computers to transfer data to each other using a phone line or cable connection.

NARU: Acronym for "Not A Registered User." Used to refer to a user whose membership in an online auction has been discontinued. People who misbehave online can be NARU'd.

Out the back door: A method of privately buying an item after an auction by dealing directly with the auction or the seller.

PC: Personal Computer. The term refers to personal computers, usually with Windows systems; does not generally refer to Macs.

Post: To enter a comment on an online bulletin board or newsgroup.

Private auction: An online auction in which the bidders' identities do not appear on the auction page. Only the seller and high bidder are notified of the final outcome of the auction, and all other bidders are anonymous. This option is rarely used. Robert Edward Auctions used it on eBay when the famous Honus Wagner card was offered in the summer of 2000. It allowed bidders to bid on a famous, expensive item and protect their identity. Others may want to use the privacy feature to spare bidders embarrassment (because the offered items are "adult," for instance).

Proxy bid: A bid placed automatically, in increments, to maintain your bid as the winning bid until it reaches your maximum.

RAM: Acronym for Random Access Memory. Hardware that stores data for running your computer. The more RAM your computer has, the faster most applications will run.

Real time: Refers to auctions that are occurring at exactly the moment in time when you are bidding online.

Reserve price: The minimum amount of money an auction will accept for an item. You can set a reserve price when you post an item for auction.

Robot: A computer program that automatically scans the Web and retrieves documents to be indexed and stored for your later retrieval. Also known as a "spider."

Search engine: A powerful software program that enables you to find information on the World Wide Web by typing descriptive words in the program's search box.

Secure browser: An Internet browser that uses encryption to scramble information such as credit card numbers.

Shill: Refers to the illegal act of bidding with the sole purpose of raising the price of an item being auctioned. Also refers to the person placing the illegal bids.

Site: *See* Web site.

Sniping: Bidding at the last minute on an item offered at an online auction, leaving little time for others to place higher bids.

Spam: Sending the same e-mail message to many people to generate business or posting the same message on many newsgroups or bulletin boards. Spam messages are often unwelcome.

SSL: Acronym for Secure Socket Layer. It is used to encrypt data, usually for monetary transactions.

Surfing: Bouncing from Web page to Web page through hyperlinks.

Traffic: The number of visitors to a particular Web page.

URL: Acronym for Uniform Resource Locator, the address that identifies the location of a Web site or a page on a site.

Web page: An HTML document containing text, images, and other online elements.

Web site: A collection of Web pages that belongs to the same person or organization.

World Wide Web: The Internet's graphics-based system that utilizes hypertext and HTML documents.

KOVELS' LIST
OF HELPFUL WEB SITES
FOR COLLECTORS

Auctions

A&A Auction Gallery	www.aaauctions.com
AcuBid	www.acubid.com
Amazon	auctions.amazon.com
Antiquorum Auctioneers	www.antiquorum.com
Auction Club	www.auctionclub.com
Auction Port	www.auctionport.com
Auctions Unlimited	www.auctions-unlimited.com
Biddington's Online Auction	www.biddingtons.com
Boekhout's Collectibles Mall	www.azww.com/mall
BoxLot	www.boxlot.com
Buy N Sell It	www.buynsellit.com
A Chip Off the Old Block	www.blocksite.com/chip
Collect It Now	www.collectitnow.com
Collecting Channel	www.collectingchannel.com
Collecting Nation	www.collectingnation.com
Collector's Sales & Service	www.antiqueglass.com
Collectors Auction Services	www.caswel.com
CyrBid	www.cyrbid.com
eBay	www.ebay.com
eDeal	www.edeal.com
eHammer	www.ehammer.com
Fainco Antique Treasures & Collectibles	www.fainco.com
FairMarket Network	auctions.fairmarket.com
Gallery Auctions	www.galleryauctions.com
Gold's Auctions	www.goldsauction.com
Haggle Online	www.haggle.com
International Collector	www.icollector.com

Joe Wasson's Online Autograph Auction . . . . .www.autografs.com

Klik-Klok Online Dutch Auction . . . . .www.klik-klok.com/auction.html

LA Modern . . . . .www.lamodern.com

LiveBid . . . . .livebid.amazon.com

Lycos Auctions . . . . .auctions.lycos.com

MastroNet . . . . .www.mastronet.com

Mile High Comics . . . . .www.milehighcomics.com

MSNauctions . . . . .auctions.msn.com

Net Collect . . . . .www.netcollect.com

Northland Auction . . . . .www.northlandauction.com

Old and Sold Antique Auction . . . . .www.oldandsold.com

OnlineAuction . . . . .www.onlineauction.com

Pottery Auction . . . . .www.potteryauction.com

Rago Arts . . . . .www.ragoarts.com

Serious Collector . . . . .www.seriouscollector.com

Skinner, Inc. . . . . .skinner.lycos.com

SoldUSA . . . . .www.soldusa.com

Sotheby's . . . . .www.sothebys.com

Swappers and Collectors .www.swappersandcollectors.com

Trade Card Auction . . . . .www.mobilia.com

Treadway Gallery . . . . .www.treadwaygallery.com

Wolf's Fine Art Auctioneers . . . . .www.ewolfs.com

World Wide Collectors Digest Auctions . . . . .www.wwcd.com

Xbid . . . . .www.xbid.com

Yahoo! Auction . . . . .auctions.yahoo.com

Auction Portals

4 Auction 4auction.4anything.com

Antiques Only . . . . .www.antiquesonly.com

The Auction Channel . . . . .www.theauctionchannel.com

Auction Ferret . . . . .www.auctionferret.com

Auction Patrol . . . . .www.auctionpatrol.com

Auction Watch . . . . .www.auctionwatch.com

Auctions Portal . . . . .www.auctions-portal.com

Bidder's Edge . . . . www.biddersedge.com

Internet Auction List . . . . www.internetauctionlist.com

iTrack . . . . www.itrack.com

RealBidder . . . . www.realbidder.com

Price Guides

Aaron's Price Guide (Star Wars) . . . . www.aaronspriceguide.com

Alley Guide (Hot Wheels) . . . . www.mobilia.com

Antique Trader's Collect (subscription) . . . . www.collect.com

Art Fact (subscription) . . . . www.artfact.com

Beckett's . . . . www.beckett.com

Bidder's Edge . . . . www.biddersedge.com

Coin Universe . . . . www.coin-universe.com

Collector Values (Steiff) . . . . www.collectorvalues.com

Comics Price Guide (subscription) . . . . www.comicspriceguide.com

Honesty Auction Tools . . . . www.honesty.com

International Arts, Antiques & Collectibles Forum . . . . www.the-forum.com

International Music Discographies . . . . www.recordmaster.com

Keen Kutter Price Guide . . . . www.solarmatrix.com/KeenKutter

Kovels' Online Price Guide . . . . **www.kovels.com**

Numis.net . . . . www.numis.net

Papa Smurf . . . . www.papasmurf.com

Pez Heads . . . . www.pezheads.org/prices

Price Radar . . . . www.priceradar.com

Prices for Antiques (subscription) www.prices4antiques.com

Roycroft . . . . www.roycroftcopper.com

Tuff Stuff . . . . www.tuffstuffonline.com

Worth Guide . . . . www.worthguide.com

Wurlitzer Juke Book Price Guide . . . . www.wurlitzer-jukebox.com/
reference-priceguide.html

Dealer Malls

Antique Alley . . . . www.antiquealley.com

Antique Antics . . . . www.antiqueantics.com

Antique-Expo . . . . .www.antique-expo.com

Antique Info Center and Cyber Mall . . . . .www.antiqueinfo.com

Antique Networking . . . . .www.antiqnet.com

Antique One www.antique1.com

Antique Plaza . . . . .www.antiqueplazaonline.com

Antique Shops USA . . . . .www.antiqueshopsusa.com

Antique Trove . . . . .www.trovenet.com

Antique World . . . . .www.antiqueworld.net

Antiques Are Simply Marvelous . . . . .www.simplymarvelous.com

Antiques Online . . . . .www.antiquesonline.com

Antiques World . . . . .www.antiquesworld.com

Bargain Hut . . . . .www.thebargainhut.com

Brass Armadillo Antique Mall . . . . .www.brassarmadillo.com

Brimfield Heart-of-the-Mart .www.brimfield-hotm.com

Buy Collectibles . . . . .www.buycollectibles.com

Classifieds 2000 (Excite classifieds) www.classifieds2000.com

Collector Online . . . . .www.collectoronline.com

Crafty Classifieds .www.ideaquest.com/ads/welcome.html

Cyber Antique Mall . . . . .www.cyberantiquemall.com

Cyber Attic . . . . .www.cyberattic.com

DG Shopper (Depression glass) .www.dgshopper.com

ForSale.com . . . . .www.forsale.com

Go Antiquing . . . . .www.goantiquing.com

International Collector . . . . .www.icollector.com

International Arts, Antiques & Collectibles Forum . . . . .www.the-forum.com

The Internet Antique Shop . . . . .www.tias.com

Kaleden . . . . .www.kaleden.com

Machine Age . . . . .www.machineage.com

Mullica Hill Merchants Association . . . . .www.mullicahill.com

New England Events Management . . . . .www.antiquefest.com

Palmer Wirfs Assoc. Ant. & Collectibles Shows . . . . .www.collect.com/palmer

Ruby Lane . . . . .www.rubylane.com

Serious Collector . . . . .www.seriouscollector.com

Southern Belle Antiques . . . . .www.southern-belle.com

Texas Antique Mall . . . . www.txantiquemall.com

World Wide Collectors Digest   . . . . .www.wwcd.com

Reference Sites

Alan's Marble Connection (repros) . . . . .www.marblealan.com/reproduc.htm

Antique . . . . .www.antique.org

Antique & Collectors Reproduction News . . . . .www.repronews.com

Antique Appeal . . . . .www.antiqueappeal.com

Antique Dealer and Collector Software . . . . .www.tinkerware.com

Antique Hot Spots . . . . .www.antiquehotspots.com

Antique Resources . . . . .www.antiqueresources.com

Antiques & Art Around Florida . . . . .www.aarf.com

Antiques Oronoco . . . . .www.antiques-oronoco.com

Auction Bytes . . . . .www.auctionbytes.com

Best Antiques & Collectibles Sites . . . . .www.computrends.com/antiquering

Better Business Bureau Online . . . . .www.bbb.org

A Chip off the Old Block (repro marbles) . . . .www.blocksite.com/mcc/alert.htm

Collecting Channel . . . . .www.collectingchannel.com

Collector Web . . . . .www.collectorweb.com

Collectors Universe . . . . .www.collectors.com

Curioscape . . . . .www.curioscape.com

eGroups . . . . .www.egroups.com

Federal Trade Commission . . . . .www.ftc.gov

History Net . . . . .www.thehistorynet.com

How Stuff Works (by Marshall Brain) . . . . .www.howstuffworks.com

Info Please . . . . .www.infoplease.com

International Arts, Antiques & Collectibles Forum . . . . .www.the-forum.com

Internet Fraud Watch . . . . .www.fraud.org/internet/intset.htm

Maloneys Online . . . . .www.maloneysonline.com

National Association of Collectors . . . . .www.collectors.org

National Consumers League . . . . .www.natlconsumersleague.org

The Official U.S. Time (atomic clock) . . . . .www.time.gov

Online Auction Users Association . . . . .www.auctionusers.org

Portobello Road . . . . .www.portobelloroad.co.uk

Real Time Antiques Market . . . . .www.rtam.com

Refdesk . . . . .www.refdesk.com

Roseville Pottery Exchange .www.ohioriverpottery.com/
roseville_exchange/roseville.html

Smithsonian: Porcelain and Pottery Marks . . . . .www.si.edu/
resource/faq/nmah/potmarks.htm

Travlang's Translating Dictionaries . . . . .dictionaries.travlang.com

The Universal Currency Converter .www.xe.net/ucc

Victoriana . . . . .www.victoriana.com

World Collectors Network . . . . .www.worldcollectorsnet.com

Yahoo Web Rings . . . . .webring.yahoo.com/rw

Your Dictionary . . . . .www.yourdictionary.com

Appraisal & Grading Services

Antique Appraisals . . . . .www.antiqueappraisals.net

Appraise It Net . . . . .www.appraiseitnet.com

The Appraiser Network . . . . .www.theappraisernetwork.com

Artisan Woodworkers . . . . .www.artworkers.com/appraisals.html

Auction Watch . . . . .www.auctionwatch.com

Beckett's . . . . .www.beckett.com

Collect It Now . . . . .www.collectitnow.com/utome_popup.html

Collecting Channel .www.collectingchannel.com

eCurator . . . . .www.ecurator.com

Epraisal . . . . .www.epraisal.com

Eppraisals . . . . .www.eppraisals.com

One of a Kind Antiques . . . . .www.oneofakindantiques.com

Professional Coin-Grading Service . . . . .www.pcgs.com

Image Hosts, Counters, Batch Loaders & Other Auction Services

Andale . . . . .www.andale.com

Auction Flow . . . . .www.auctionflow.com

Auction Image . . . . .www.auctionimage.com

Auction Patrol . . . . .www.auctionpatrol.com

Auction Pix . . . . .www.auctionpix.com
Auction Rover . . . . .www.auctionrover.com
Auction Watch . . . . .www.auctionwatch.com
Cataloging by Columbus . . . . .www.columbuscat.com
eDisplay . . . . .www.edisplay.com
ePho.com . . . . .www.epho.com
ePoster 2000 . . . . .www.auctionposter.com
Honesty Auction Tools . . . . .www.honesty.com
Internet Pictures Corp. . . . . .www.ipix.com
Manage Auctions . . . . .www.manageauctions.com
Photo Point . . . . .www.photopoint.com
Picture This . . . . .www.picturethiss.com
Pix Host . . . . .www.pixhost.com
Pix Plus . . . . .www.pixplus.com
Pongo Tutorials . . . . .www.pongo.com
Show Your Stuff . . . . .www.zinasplace.com/showyourstuff
SSI Image Hosting . . . . .www.ssiimage.com

Escrow and Mediation Services

Escrow.com . . . . .www.escrow.com
iEscrow . . . . .www.iescrow.com
Internet Clearing Corporation . . . . .www.internetclearing.com
Square Trade . . . . .www.squaretrade.com
Web Trade Insure . . . . .www.webtradeinsure.com

Secure Payment Services

Bid Pay . . . . .www.bidpay.com
Billpoint . . . . .www.billpoint.com
Pay Me . . . . .www.payme.com
Pay Pal . . . . .www.paypal.com
Western Union . . . . .www.westernunion.com
Yahoo PayDirect . . . . .paydirect.yahoo.com

Other Helpful Sites for Collectors

Cricket, Jr. (bid manager) . . . . .www.worldint.com/journeys/eccles/cricketjr

Cyber Source (Internet Fraud Screen) . . . . .www.cybersource.com

eSnipe (bid manager) . . . . .www.esnipe.com

eStamp . . . . .www.estamp.com

eWanted (reverse auction) . . . . .www.ewanted.com

imandi (reverse auction) . . . . .www.imandi.com

Mailboxes Etc. . . . . .www.mbe.com

PakMail (shipping unusual shapes & sizes) . . . . .www.pakmail.com

Respond (e-mail requests for items) .www.respond.com

Reverse Auction . . . . .www.reverseauction.com

ShipSmart . . . . .www.shipsmart.com

Stamps . . . . .www.stamps.com

United Parcel Service . . . . .www.ups.com

United States Postal Service . . . . .www.usps.com

Virtual Feedback . . . . .www.virtualfeedback.com

Barter Sites

A Barter Site . . . . .www.abartersite.com

Big Vine . . . . .www.bigvine.com

Exchange Anything . . . . .www.exchangeanything.com

Express Barter . . . . .www.expressbarter.com

IntelliBarter . . . . .www.intellibarter

Mr. Swap . . . . .www.mrswap.com

Swap and Save . . . . .www.swapandsave.com

SwitcHouse . . . . .www.switchouse.com

Web Swap . . . . .www.webswap.com

Yes Swap . . . . .www.yesswap.com

NOTES

If you are like us, you misplace your user ID and password for various sites.
Jot them below, and you'll always have them handy.

Web Address	User ID	Password	Comments

INDEX

KOVELS ORDER FORM

SEND ORDERS & INQUIRIES TO: **CROWN PUBLISHERS**
c/o: **RANDOM HOUSE, 400 HAHN ROAD,**
   WESTMINSTER, MD 21157 ATTN: **ORDER DEPARTMENT**
WEBSITE: www.randomhouse.com

SALES & TITLE INFORMATION:
1-800-733-3000

FOR ORDER ENTRY:
FAX# 1-800-659-2436

NAME_____

ADDRESS _____

CITY & STATE _____ ZIP _____

Please send me the following books:

ITEM NO.	QTY.	TITLE		PRICE	TOTAL
0-609-80571-1	___	Kovels' Antiques & Collectibles Price List —33rd Edition	PAPER	$15.95	_____
0-517-70137-5	___	Dictionary of Marks—Pottery and Porcelain	HARDCOVER	$17.00	_____
0-517-55914-5	___	Kovels' New Dictionary of Marks	HARDCOVER	$19.00	_____
0-517-56882-9	___	Kovels' American Silver Marks	HARDCOVER	$40.00	_____
0-609-80757-9	___	Kovels' Bid, Buy, and Sell Online	PAPER	$14.00	_____
0-609-80312-3	___	Kovels' Bottles Price List—11th Edition	PAPER	$16.00	_____
0-609-80310-7	___	Kovels' Depression Glass & Dinnerware Price List —6th Edition	PAPER	$16.00	_____
0-517-57806-9	___	Kovels' Know Your Antiques, Revised and Updated	PAPER	$17.00	_____
0-517-58840-4	___	Kovels' Know Your Collectibles, Updated	PAPER	$16.00	_____
0-517-88381-3	___	Kovels' Quick Tips: 799 Helpful Hints on How to Care for Your Collectibles	PAPER	$12.00	_____
0-609-60168-7	___	The Label Made Me Buy It: From Aunt Jemima to Zonkers	HARDCOVER	$40.00	_____
0-609-80417-0	___	Kovels' Yellow Pages: A Collector's Directory of Names, Addresses, Telephone and Fax Numbers, E-Mail, and Internet Addresses to Make Selling, Fixing, and Pricing Your Antiques and Collectibles Easy	PAPER	$18.00	_____
	___	TOTAL ITEMS	TOTAL RETAIL VALUE		_____

CHECK OR MONEY ORDER ENCLOSED
MADE PAYABLE TO CROWN PUBLISHERS
or telephone 1-800-733-3000
(No cash or stamps, please)

Shipping & Handling
Charge (per order) $5.50

Please add applicable sales tax. _____

TOTAL AMOUNT DUE $_____

CHARGE: ☐ MasterCard ☐ Visa ☐ American Express
Account Number (include all digits) Expires: MO.___ YR.___

_____

PRICES SUBJECT TO CHANGE
WITHOUT NOTICE.
If a more recent edition of a price list
has been published at the same price,
it will be sent instead of the old edition.

Thank you for your order

Signature

"As millions already know,
any book carrying the Kovel byline will be
as reliable, informative, and fact~filled
as any collector could wish."

—*AMERICAN COUNTRY*

Ralph and Terry Kovel, America's antiques and collectibles experts, have written more than 80 books. Among them are:

Kovels' Antiques & Collectibles Price List—33rd Edition
0-609-80571-1. $15.95 paper

Kovels' Bottles Price List—11th Edition
0-609-80312-3. $16.00 paper

Kovels' Depression Glass & Dinnerware Price List—6th Edition
0-609-80310-7. $16.00 paper

Kovels' New Dictionary of Marks
0-517-55914-5. $19.00 hardcover

Kovels' Know Your Antiques
0-517-57806-9. $17.00 paper

Kovels' Know Your Collectibles
0-517-58840-4. $16.00 paper

AVAILABLE WHEREVER BOOKS ARE SOLD.